New edition

Listening

Teacher's Book

Colin Campbell and Jonathan Smith

ISLC
International Study
and Language Centre

University of
Reading

Garnet
EDUCATION

Credits

Published by
Garnet Publishing Ltd.
8 Southern Court
South Street
Reading RG1 4QS, UK

This edition first published 2012

ISBN: 978 1 90861 434 6

British Library Cataloguing-in-Publication Data
A catalogue record for this book is available from the British Library.

Production

Project manager:	Kate Kemp
Project consultant:	Fiona McGarry
Editorial team:	Fiona Aisch, Kate Kemp, Sue Coll, Clare Roberts, Kayleigh Buller
Art director:	Mike Hinks
Design and layout:	Simon Ellway, Ian Lansley, Maddy Lane

Every effort has been made to trace copyright holders and we apologize in advance for any unintentional omissions. We will be happy to insert the appropriate acknowledgements in any subsequent editions.

Printed and bound in Lebanon by International Press: interpress@int-press.com

Contents

c

Book map

	Unit title and topics	Skills focus	Microskills
1	**Listening and lectures** *Problems of listening* *Differences between academic cultures*	■ Listening in different languages ■ Issues in understanding spoken English ■ Listening to lectures	
2	**Introductions to lectures** *Migration* *Britain and the European Monetary Union* *Globalization* *Magistrates' courts*	■ Thinking about introductions ■ Functions and language of lecture introductions ■ Listening to lecture introductions	■ Word stress
3	**Identifying key ideas in lectures** *Franchising*	■ Thinking about key ideas ■ Identifying key points in a lecture ■ Distinguishing key points from examples ■ Signposting and highlighting key points	■ Word families (1)
4	**Note-taking: Part 1** *Britain's traffic problems* *The East-Asian economic miracle*	■ Reasons for taking notes ■ Principles of note-taking ■ Note-taking practice	■ Sentence stress
5	**Note-taking: Part 2** *Language learning* *Changes in the world economy* *Health in the UK*	■ Returning to your notes ■ Using abbreviations and symbols ■ Organizing your notes	■ Word boundaries
6	**Introducing new terminology** *Embedded words* *European Union: regulations and directives* *Market dominance and monopoly*	■ Introducing new terminology ■ Introducing terms and concepts	■ Weak forms of function words
7	**What lecturers do in lectures** *Doing market research* *Social learning* *Contestable markets*	■ Macrostructure of lectures	■ Word families (2)
8	**Digressions** *Social learning* *Questionnaire design* *Integrated rural development*	■ Reasons for digressions ■ Identifying digressions	■ Common expressions in lectures

i Introduction

Aims of the course

The purpose of this book is to help students better understand spoken English, particularly the spoken English of academic lectures, as well as to help them develop their note-taking skills while listening.

Processes in listening comprehension

Researchers into the processes involved in listening comprehension have distinguished between 'bottom-up' decoding of spoken language and the application of 'top-down' processing, which involves deploying, for example, understanding of context and world knowledge. Flowerdew (1994) argues that these terms may be misleading in that they suggest a hierarchical, two-way model for listening comprehension for which there is no empirical basis. He states that while scholars accept that listening comprehension involves a variety of processes, all of which interact, it is not possible to determine and describe *how* they interact.

Flowerdew refers to a more commonly accepted conceptualization of listening comprehension as a 'two-stage process; the first stage consisting of purely linguistic processing and the second of application of the results of this linguistic processing to background knowledge and context'. Significantly, he points out that when international students are given training in understanding academic lectures, the emphasis tends to be on developing the 'higher-level' skills, the assumption being that they have already developed skills in decoding spoken language to a sufficient level.

Students may often be able to fill in some of the gaps in their decoding of spoken language by applying 'higher-level' skills. However, the authors' experiences of teaching on courses aimed at preparing students for academic study in the UK have shown that many students are unable to decode enough of the stream of natural speech to be able to do so.

For this reason, this book focuses on both: macroskills, the 'higher-level' skills such as recognizing the purpose and structure of a lecture; and microskills, the skills involved in linguistic processing which include, for example, recognizing weak forms and word boundaries. Each unit (apart from Unit 1) is organized so that macroskills work precedes microskills work, but this is not intended to suggest that one has greater importance than the other.

The balance of work on these two different types of skills may depend on the level of the group you are teaching and the stage in the course; students with stronger language knowledge may need less work on microskills.

Microskills

Field (2003) identifies a number of problems students may have decoding natural speech. Students may be familiar with the spoken form of a word, but may attribute the wrong sense to it in a particular context. They may fail to recognize a phonetic variant of a word they know, or even fail to recognize a word they know in the written form. In addition, they may be unable to segment the word out of a piece of natural speech. Field argues that 'many high-level breakdowns in communication originate in low-level errors' (2003).

The microskills sections focus on some of these areas of difficulty in decoding spoken language. The problem of recognizing words students may know in the written form is addressed in Units 2, 3 and 7, where the issue of word stress and its effect on weakening other syllables in the word are discussed, as is the effect of word-stress patterns in word families. Units 4, 5 and 6 look at a number of issues that cause students problems in segmenting natural speech: the effects of stress-timing in compressing stretches of language; weak forms of function words; linking, intrusion, assimilation on word boundaries. These are areas normally covered in work on pronunciation; this book examines them from the listener's perspective.

Macroskills

Even though students may not have difficulty decoding, they may have problems following argumentation or understanding the relationships between ideas. Olsen and Huckin (1990) found that international students often have difficulties following argumentation that is developed over more complex discourse structures than they are used to. Tauroza and Allison (in Flowerdew, 1994) reported that students had difficulties with main points when there was a departure from the expected discourse structure of the lecture.

The macroskills sections focus on areas such as understanding the different purposes of lectures, and common macrostructures of lectures; recognizing the functions of language in the context of a lecture; identifying key ideas and distinguishing digression from the main thread of the argument.

Note-taking

Research into note-taking has focused on areas such as the reasons for taking notes (Dunkel & Davy, 1989), techniques for taking notes (Rost, 1990) and the relationship between the quality of notes and successful recall of lecture information at a later date (Chaudron, Loschky & Cook, 1994). The activities in this book emphasize the personal nature of notes and present a range of techniques for saving time and showing the relationships between ideas (e.g., using abbreviations and symbols). They also stress the importance of being able to reconstruct notes when returning to them after some time. In addition, linear and mind-mapping approaches to note-taking are related to both the macrostructure of the lecture and students' preferred learning styles.

Lecturing style and discourse structure

Flowerdew (1994), summarizing studies by other researchers, identifies differences in lecturing style in terms of the extent to which the speaker reads from a script or extemporizes, and the degree of interaction with the audience. The suggestion is that an 'informal, conversational style, based on notes or handouts is probably the predominant mode of lecture presentation'.

Many of the recordings accompanying this book have been adapted from extracts taken from authentic lectures delivered to undergraduate and postgraduate audiences at the University of Reading, and which form part of the BASE (British Academic Spoken English) corpus (www2.warwick.ac.uk/fac/soc/celte/research/base/). The selection of suitable lecture extracts attempts to ensure accessibility of topic and a wide range of subject areas in the social sciences, physical sciences and humanities. However, it is also hoped that they represent a range of lecturing styles, through the choice of scripts and style of delivery on the part of the actors on the DVD. While we cannot claim that the DVD recordings are authentic, we believe we have achieved a good compromise between authenticity and the need to produce recordings that are accessible to learners.

The authors' informal analysis of lectures from the BASE corpus has revealed the following common features of discourse in lectures:

- lengthy introductions to lectures, which include a lot of discussion around course management and contextualization before the main focus of the lecture begins
- substantial use of informal and idiomatic language by lecturers
- considerable variation in the amount of digression by lecturers
- less use of (and consistency in the use of) discourse markers to organize information than we might have expected

These findings have been taken into account in the design of the learning materials. There is, for example, less emphasis on listening for discourse markers as a means of identifying key ideas to note down, and more emphasis on understanding the relationships between ideas, and the use of emphatic stress, pausing and reference to visual aids.

Student expectations

Students' attitudes towards the development of listening skills will be partly shaped by their previous learning experiences. Many students will come from an educational background in which listening skills work has focused on microskills and close understanding. Typical classroom activities may have included the use of gapped texts, dictation and exposition of the text by the teacher. The idea of varying listening strategies according to the purpose for listening is likely to be unfamiliar, and some students may find it unsatisfactory to leave a listening text with the sense that they have only 'understood' the general idea, or a few key points. Moreover, some students tend to view listening texts principally as contexts in which they can develop language knowledge, by focusing on new vocabulary or examples of grammatical structures. If this is the case, then setting follow-up learning tasks, focusing on close understanding, may provide one way to give reassurance for such students. These tasks can be based round the use of transcripts, and may also be set for homework.

Techniques for developing listening skills

- Ensure that there is some kind of preparation for each listening activity. This might range from a brief activity in which students predict issues they expect to hear discussed, to something more detailed, such as a reading and discussion activity. In some cases pre-listening activities are provided in the Course Book, and in other cases you will find suggestions in this Teacher's Book.
- Be prepared to play a recording twice (or more) for students to perform the task. A typical procedure might be as follows:
  1. play the recording
  2. students compare their notes or answers in pairs
  3. play the recording a second time for students to add anything they missed the first time, or to check with their partner on anything they disagreed over
  4. students compare their notes again
  5. elicit answers from students
- The recordings provide students with practice in listening to a range of lecturing styles and accents, and to variation in pace and tonal range. However, don't forget that you have the option of using your own voice from time to time to deliver texts, by reading from the transcripts. This might be appropriate if you feel that aspects of the recorded voice, rather than the content, are preventing students from understanding texts. One useful variation on this approach is to play the authentic recording the first time, check what students have understood and then read out the transcript to the students.
- When you use the recordings, you will certainly find that there are short sections which cause students difficulty. In many cases, either students may be able to infer the general meaning from the context, or it may be that full comprehension is not essential for the listening purpose. In these cases, you can simply move on. However, in some cases these sections may include key ideas, without which students are unable to gain enough sense of the text as a whole, and you will have to do some more focused 'close' listening work.

Close listening work

Depending on the context, you will need to draw on a range of techniques:

- Find the section which is causing students difficulty, and play it again and again, building up meaning between plays.
- Try to establish why students are having problems understanding. It may be that:
  - they can't recognize individual word forms
  - they can't recognize where one word ends and another begins
  - they recognize individual words, but do not assign them the correct meaning in a particular context
  - they understand the individual words, but they don't understand how they are related to one another to construct meaning
  - they understand the meaning of the complete utterance, but can't relate it to the rest of the text
- If necessary, build up sections of the listening text on the board. Elicit from students the words they recognize and write them up, leaving gaps for any words/phrases that they do not recognize. You can also indicate how many words are missing in each gap, by representing each missing word with underlining, *e.g., … the increase _____ _____ _____ causes several problems* … Again, reading the section yourself (rather than playing the recording) may help students recognize words.
- The previous technique focuses on the form of words. Students sometimes get over-focused on trying to match the stream of sounds they hear to their repertoire of vocabulary, and neglect the meaning. As an example, in a lecture extract about the advantages of different forms of waste disposal, students thought they heard *… (incineration of waste) reduces its value by 90 per cent …* The teacher pointed out that a reduction in value could not be an advantage, and then asked students to visualize a quantity of waste that is put in a landfill compared with the same quantity after incineration. After a certain amount of prompting, some students arrived at the intended meaning: *… reduces its volume by 90 per cent.* Students will need to be reminded regularly to deploy their world knowledge to make sense of what they hear, and may need some guidance towards understanding.

Checking note-taking activities

Sample notes are provided for the note-taking activities. They have not been called Model answers, because that suggests they are the perfection towards which students should be striving, and that is *not* the case. They do include what are judged to be the key points, and they are intended to be accurate, but they are selective and personal, so students may well be justified in noting down different ideas.

When it comes to checking completion of the note-taking activities, there is a range of options. Those at the top of the list below maximize student input.

- Pairs of students collate their notes onto a visual aid, for discussion. If you are working with a long recording, you can assign different sections to different pairs.
- Individual students write their notes on the board. Students then discuss the focus and accuracy of the notes.
- Elicit the students' notes from them and write them up on the board.
- Elicit the students' notes orally.
- Project the sample notes, and have students compare their own notes with them.

We recommend that you vary your approach to checking the note-taking activities, but that you ensure that students do most of the work, by using some of the techniques at the top of the list.

Transcripts

Depending on the needs of your own class, you may feel it appropriate to provide follow-up microskills work on certain texts. One way of doing this is to work with the transcripts, which are located at the end of both the Course Book and Teacher's Book. You could possibly create gap-fill activities focusing on stretches of language students might have difficulty decoding.

In the microskills sections there are a number of gapped transcripts, whose completed versions are not included in the transcripts section at the back of the book. The gapped transcripts can be found as photocopiable handouts at the end of the relevant unit. Other photocopiable handouts can also be found at the end of the units. Note that all the photocopiable materials in this book are also available as downloadable files in the teacher's section of the EAS website – **www.englishforacademicstudy.com.**

If you have a difficult text, it is worth playing through sections of the recording while students read the transcript (*after* the note-taking activity) and then trying to identify what is causing the difficulty, e.g., problems with word boundaries, unfamiliar key vocabulary, unclear sense relationships.

Unit summaries

These provide an opportunity for the students to reflect on what they have done at the end of each unit. You may wish students to complete the unit summaries in class or in their own time. If students complete them out of class, make sure you find time to discuss what they have done.

Other features

Glossary: Located at the end of the Course Book, this contains a useful list of terms that the students will need to know during the course.

Sound advice: These sections appear in the body of the student material, and are designed to highlight important information related to the listening skill that will help students to complete the tasks.

Study tips: These contain additional information that can be used by students as a ready-reference to a range of study issues related to the listening skill.

Progression and differentation

The Course Book is designed so that tasks and texts become more challenging as students work through the materials. In general, the earlier units are characterized by shorter texts, scripted recordings and familiar topics, and the later ones are charactized by longer texts, transcribed from authentic lecture recordings, and by more demanding topics.

Do not feel you have to do all of the microskills practice activities. Some of them are marked *Easy* and others *More demanding*, and you can choose to drop these depending on the general level of your class. Alternatively, you could set these for homework or optional consolidation.

References

Chaudron, C., Loschky, L., & Cook, J. (1994). Second language listening comprehension and lecture note-taking. In J. Flowerdew (Ed.), *Academic listening: Research perspectives* (pp. 55–74). Cambridge: Cambridge University Press.

Dunkel, P., & Davy, S. (1989). The heuristic of lecture note-taking: Perceptions of American and international students regarding the value and practice of note-taking. *English for Specific Purposes, 8*(1), 33–50.

Field, J. (2003). Promoting perception: Lexical segmentation in L2 listening. *ELT Journal, 57*(4), 325–333.

Flowerdew, J. (1994). Research of relevance to second language lecture comprehension: An overview. In J. Flowerdew (Ed.), *Academic listening: Research perspectives* (pp. 7–30). Cambridge: Cambridge University Press.

Olsen, L. A., & Huckin, T. N. (1990). Point-driven understanding in engineering lecture comprehension. *English for Specific Purposes, 9*(1), 33–47.

Rost, M. (1990). *Listening in language learning*. London: Longman.

Tauroza, S., & Allison, D. (1994). Expectation-driven understanding in information systems lecture comprehension. In J. Flowerdew (Ed.), *Academic listening: Research perspectives* (pp. 35–54). Cambridge: Cambridge University Press.

Route through the materials

The *EAS: Listening* material can either be used in combination with other titles in the EAS series or as a stand-alone listening course. The books are designed for international students of English intending to pursue academic study in an English-speaking environment, whose IELTS level is between 5.0 and 7.5. However, much of the material can be adapted for use with less proficient students.

In general, less proficient students will find the early units easier to cope with, and if they still have problems decoding natural connected speech, will need to do many of the microskills activities at the end of each unit.

Conversely, it may be appropriate to focus on the more demanding later units when teaching students with stronger listening skills, and these students may need less work on microskills.

On pages 11 and 12 are a number of suggested routes through the book, depending on the length of the course and the number of teaching hours required to reach the minimum university entrance level. These are based on two 90-minute lessons per week. The amount of work given to students to be completed outside class may vary; some tasks need to be covered in class, while others can be set for homework to consolidate or further practice points covered in class.

Note: Non-contact hours = homework and independent study related to the materials.

Suggested route for 16-week course

Week	Contact hours	Non-contact hours	Unit
1	3	2	Unit 1
2	3	2	Unit 2
3	3	2	Unit 2
4	3	2	Unit 3
5	3	2	Unit 3
6	3	2	Unit 3
7	3	2	Unit 4
8	3	2	Unit 4
9	3	2	Unit 5
10	3	2	Unit 5
11	3	2	Unit 6
12	3	2	Unit 6
13	3	2	Unit 7
14	3	2	Unit 7
15	3	2	Unit 8
16	3	2	Unit 8

Suggested route for 11-week course

Week	Contact hours	Non-contact hours	Unit
1	3	2	Unit 1
2	3	2	Unit 2
3	3	2	Unit 2
4	3	2	Unit 3
5	3	2	Unit 3
6	3	2	Unit 4
7	3	2	Unit 5
8	3	2	Unit 5
9	3	2	Unit 6
10	3	2	Unit 6
11	3	2	Unit 7

Suggested route for 8-week course

Week	Contact hours	Non-contact hours	Unit
1	3	2	Unit 1
2	3	2	Unit 2
3	3	2	Unit 2
4	3	2	Unit 3
5	3	2	Unit 3
6	3	2	Unit 4
7	3	2	Unit 5
8	3	2	Unit 6

Suggested route for 5-week course

Week	Contact hours	Non-contact hours	Unit
1	1.5	1	Unit 1
	1.5	2	Unit 2
2	3	2	Unit 3
3	3	2	Unit 4
4	3	2	Unit 5
5	3	2	Unit 6

1 Listening and lectures

In this unit students will:
- discuss the different situations in which they have to listen
- identify what factors influence their ability to understand
- learn about features of lectures in different academic cultures

Task 1 | Listening in different languages

The aim of this task is to get students thinking about the different types of listening, and about the notion that we vary our listening strategies according to what we are listening to.

1.1 You can either do this task as a discussion among the whole class, or in pairs/small groups before summarizing with the whole class.

Students should come up with some of the following points.
- When you are involved in a conversation, you can check your understanding, while you cannot for the other contexts. This means that you probably do not need to concentrate as hard.
- When people listen to the radio, they tend to tune in and out depending on how interested they are in the topic. There may well be a difference in attention level between listening to music on the radio while you do the ironing, and listening to a penalty shoot-out involving your favourite football team.
- When you listen to announcements at a railway station, you are generally listening for specific information; you are probably listening for your destination, the platform number, arrival time, and whether or not your train is on time.
- When listening to an academic lecture, there is likely to be more 'close listening' than for the other contexts, but, in fact, students will be applying different skills at different points in the lecture. They might be listening for specific information at the beginning if, for example, they expect to hear a deadline for an assignment; they might 'tune out' and listen for gist during a digression.

For lower-level students or less talkative groups, you could write the above notes on cards and ask students to match them to the situations.

Task 2 | Understanding spoken English

The aim of this task to is to highlight the problems of listening for students while they discuss points and listen to each other.

2.1 Students are likely to cite factors like unfamiliar vocabulary, accent and lack of listening practice in their previous education as factors causing problems when listening to English.

This activity could be done as a class questionnaire to increase the background noise, and range of accents, and to focus the students' listening.

2.2   ▶ **CD1: 1** This listening activity raises some of the fairly predictable issues affecting comprehension, and then goes on to look at two specific problems of decoding spoken English. In later units there will be more detailed analysis and practice recognizing unfamiliar word forms and word boundaries.

After students have read the questions, play Track 1.

Answers:

1. The teacher discusses the factor of the speed at which someone is speaking. She does not discuss background noise.

2. She also talks about topic and specialized vocabulary as factors affecting comprehension.

3. The two additional problems she discusses:
   - the problem of word boundaries (understanding where one word ends and another begins)
   - recognizing words pronounced in an unexpected way

Students who have studied English primarily through the written medium are likely to have listening problems and fail to recognize words or phrases that they would otherwise recognize in the written form.

2.3   ▶ **CD1: 2** In the second part of the talk, the teacher illustrates the two problems she has introduced. Before you play Track 2, check that students understand they have to write down a phrase which is dictated during the talk.

After you have played Track 2, elicit the phrase *words they hear in natural speech* and write it on the board.

Ask students to explain why this phrase is difficult to decode. Using the written phrase on the board, guide the students to the following responses: the linking (*hear‿in‿natural*) may cause difficulties, in addition to the elided vowel in *natural* /nætʃrəl/.

Extension activity
Discuss this question as a class, or with weaker groups explain how the phrase in 2.3 illustrates the lecture.

2.4   ▶ **CD1: 3** You may need to play Track 3 two or three times before students complete the excerpt. Students can either check their answers by referring to the transcript in the Course Book, or you can elicit the answers onto the board or a visual aid showing the gapped text (see Appendix 1a, page 17).

Answers:
So what is the solution to these two problems? Well, firstly, you need to get as much practice listening to natural speech as possible. Listen to extracts from lectures and try to develop your understanding of how words and phrases are really pronounced, not how you expect them to be pronounced. And secondly, you need to accept that when you listen you may misunderstand what is being said. So you need to be ready to change your mind about your understanding of the meaning, if what you hear doesn't make sense compared to what you understood before. And this means taking a flexible, open-minded approach to listening.

2.5   Focus the students' attention on the words they misheard or did not hear at all. Try to get them to explain why they had problems. Did they have problems identifying word boundaries? Were there words they knew in the written form but did not recognize in the spoken form?

Make it clear that, during the course, the microskills work will focus on some of the problems of decoding.

For lower-level groups, scaffold this activity by giving students a list of possible answers to the questions for them to discuss in groups.

| Task 3 | Listening to lectures |

The aim of this task is to raise awareness of the variety of lecture styles across cultures.

This talk is based on a tracking study (where a sample of students were followed for a period of time) carried out by the speaker. It is important to demonstrate to students that they will have to adjust to a system where the lecture delivers less of the course content than they may be used to; they will have to do a lot more background reading around the lectures. Students will also have to recognize for themselves what the important points are.

3.1 Check what students understand by the term *lecture* and that students have attended lectures elsewhere. If you have a class that includes a large proportion of students who will be studying at a university for the first time, then they probably will not be able to discuss the topics in Ex 3.1. If this is the case, it might be better to describe what kind of lectures they might be attending in an English-speaking institution:

- generally between 45 and 90 minutes' long
- traditional lecture (questions at the end) *vs* 'interactive' lecture (questions at any point)
- lecturer generally speaks from notes, but occasionally lectures are fully scripted or delivered from memory
- visual support (e.g., PowerPoint, handouts, none)

You could use the information above as a true/false activity.

3.2 ▶ **CD1: 4 Sample notes (see Appendix 1b, page 18):**
- *Main interest = diff bet Ch & Br ac culture esp. lectures – how organized/ presented + role of lecturers*
- *Info from: tracking study w/ Ch sts – PG Uni of Reading Interviews w/ each st every term*
- *The survey small sample – 12 students.*

3.3 When students have discussed these questions in pairs, elicit ways of writing down the information concisely, e.g., omitting function words, using key words and symbols. Show students the sample notes and highlight the features of note-taking. Tell the students that they will learn more about abbreviations and symbols in later units.

3.4 Students could predict the differences as a pre-reading task. If you have Chinese students, they could tell other nationalities what lectures are like in their experience.

▶ **CD1: 5 Sample notes (see Appendix 1c, page 19):**

China	UK
- a lot of course content delivered through lectures - lecture information sufficient to pass exams/course - not interactive – no questions/comments from students - lecturer points out key points - based on one course book	- most course content not delivered through lectures - lectures give overview or background info - students have to read around lectures - can be very interactive – depends on number of students

3.5   Students compare their notes and discuss ways of reducing the word count of their notes. With higher-level groups you could give them a word limit for each idea/point.

3.6   You may wish to give students time individually to review their notes and think about their answers to the questions before discussing in groups.

If you do not have students from China, omit question 1. The discussion can be organized in mixed-nationality groups.

After the discussion, ask students to report back to the whole class. You may wish to focus on their answers to questions 5 and 6 to help them prepare for the lecture cycle and ultimately their own academic courses. You may also want to check that they have mentioned the following:

- reading any handouts given before the lectures
- reviewing own notes
- checking notes with peers
- discussing the content with peers, etc.

With less talkative groups, this activity could be done as a class survey. After a specific time for questioning, pairs could discuss what they found out from their class members.

Unit summary

You may wish the students to complete the unit summaries in class or in their own time. If they complete them out of class, make sure you get some feedback during class time. Whatever you choose, it might be beneficial to set up some of the activities in class, either to clarify what to do, or to help students start thinking about the topics.

Some of the items can be done individually and others are best done in pairs or groups. When working outside the classroom, encourage students to find the time to meet with others and complete any pair or group activities.

The activities in Unit 1 are based mainly around student reflection. Encourage them to think carefully about the way they answer and to share their conclusions with other students.

You could set up reflection groups in the class and make sure students record their discussions in some way. You can encourage students to be reflective in creative ways such as diaries, blogs, visual images, reflective journals, audio/video. This type of reflection does not need to be teacher-led.

Appendix 1a

Answers:

So what is the solution to these two problems? Well, firstly, you need to get as much practice listening to natural speech as possible. Listen to _____ and try to develop your understanding of how words and phrases are really pronounced, not how you _____ pronounced. And secondly, you need to accept that when you listen you may misunderstand what is being said. So you need to be ready to _____ about your understanding of the meaning, if what you hear _____ compared to what you understood before. And this means taking a flexible, open-minded approach to listening.

- Main interest = diff bet Ch & Br ac culture esp. lectures – how organized/ presented + role of lecturers

- Info from: tracking study w/ Ch sts – PG Uni of Reading Interviews w/ each st every term

- The survey small sample – 12 students.

PHOTOCOPIABLE

Appendix 1c

China	UK
■ a lot of course content delivered through lectures	■ most course content not delivered through lectures
■ lecture information sufficient to pass exams/course	■ lectures give overview or background info
■ not interactive – no questions/ comments from students	■ students have to read around lectures
■ lecturer points out key points	■ can be very interactive – depends on number of students
■ based on one course book	

PHOTOCOPIABLE

2 Introductions to lectures

In this unit students will:

- look at how a lecture introduction can help them to understand the lecture better
- practise making notes on introductions to lectures
- learn how to recognize words that may be pronounced differently from the way they expect them to be

Task 1 Thinking about introductions

The aim of this task is simply to give you an idea of the students' level of awareness of the content and organization of academic lectures.

1.1 If students have already attended lectures, you may like to begin by asking them to recall what the lecturer(s) did in lecture introductions.

You may also like to get students to think about introductions in essays and presentations, and to discuss what these have in common and what may be different. Elicit their own ideas and summarize them on the board for later comparison with the list in Task 2.

1.2 Students should be aware that:
- some lecturers use visuals, PowerPoint slides or handouts to give an overview of their lecture
- some speakers structure lectures verbally by giving an overview in the introduction, and/or by using 'transition language' to move from one section to another

1.3 With lower-level groups, you may need to guide students to the answers through *yes/no* concept-check questions such as: *Did Student 1 think the lecture was about migration to the UK? Was the migration from the USA?*, etc.

Answers:
Student 1 thought the lecture was about migration from the EU to the UK. Student 2 thought it was about internal migration in the UK.

1.4 Students should check their answers in groups/pairs.

▶ **CD1: 6** The lecturer refers to EU migration as a contemporary phenomenon, but then goes on to say that she is going to focus on internal migration – *that's not the type of migration I want to look at today. What I want to look at is internal migration.* Student 1 does not seem to have recognized the contrast.

Answers:
1. Student 2.
2. Because the lecturer mentioned EU migration first.
3. *What I want to look at is …*

You may also want to draw students' attention to the use of *this discussion* and *However, that's not the type of migration that I want to look at today* in the transcript as clues to the topic of the lecture.

| Task 2 | Functions and language of lecture introductions |

The aim of this task is to highlight the functions of lecture introductions and the language used to express them.

Note: To save time, you could set these activities for homework

2.1   **a.**   Have students read through the list of functions in the left-hand column, and ask whether any of them match items that arose in Ex 1.1 and 1.2.

b.   Students should do this exercise in the same groups/pairs as in Ex 1.4.

Answers:

1.	b	**4.**	c	**7.**	f
2.	g	**5.**	d	**8.**	h
3.	i	**6.**	a	**9.**	e

As a follow–up, you may want to look at the language of the statements in more detail, examining the grammatical and lexical features.

| Task 3 | Listening to lecture introductions |

The aim of this task is to put Task 2 into context using lecture examples.

3.1– ▶ **CD1: 7–CD1: 9** For each of the three introductions you may wish to follow the same
3.6   pattern: students discuss the pre-listening questions in pairs or small groups and then check in plenary mode; check students understand the key vocabulary; after listening, they discuss which of the functions from the checklist appear in the introduction.

Answers:

3.1 **1.** The European Monetary Union.

2. Austria, Belgium, Cyprus, Estonia, Finland, France, Germany, Greece, Ireland, Italy, Luxembourg, Malta, the Netherlands, Portugal, Slovakia, Slovenia and Spain.

3. Answers depend on students.

3.2 The lecturer uses the following techniques from the checklist: 3, 5 and 8.

3.3 Answers 1–3 depend on students.

3.4 The lecturer uses the following techniques from the checklist:

1. Limiting the scope of the lecture.

2. Previewing the structure of the lecture.

3. Giving background information.

4. Explaining his own interest in the topic (he has written a book on the subject).

3.5 Answers 1–2 depend on students.

3.6 The lecturer uses the following techniques from the checklist:

1. Limiting the scope of the lecture.

5. Giving background information.

Task 4   Microskills: Word stress

This task focuses on word stress and the effect it has on the pronunciation of unstressed syllables in words.

Students may have difficulty understanding words beginning with an unstressed syllable, because they expect to hear a different vowel sound. For example, in the first syllables of *consume* and *assist* they may expect to hear two different vowel sounds, and may not expect to hear /ə/. In words beginning with an unstressed syllable, the vowel sound may be /ə/ or /ɪ/.

4.1   ▶ **CD1: 10** This exercise is aimed at sensitizing students to the issue. If students knew the words already, but failed to recognize them, try to establish why through a post-listening discussion or by listening to and reading the transcript. For example, linking of words may cause problems or students may not recognize *adopted* because they expect a different pronunciation or they do not hear the initial /ə/ or /ɪ/.

Answers:

However, <u>as the title of my lecture suggests,</u> I am going to spend most of the time today talking about why Britain <u>did not adopt the Euro</u>, and what that said, and still says, about Britain's attitude in general to membership of the European Union.

4.2   ▶ **CD1: 11** Check the pronunciation with students; if necessary, model the pronunciation yourself.

Answers:

So, for example, in the case of family break-up, it would involve making parental contact orders where the parents can't agree on how much <u>contact</u> time each parent should have with the child.

What we are mainly <u>concerned</u> with today is the criminal court, and that is what I am going to spend most of my time talking about this morning.

1. *contact* /ˈkɒntækt/; *concerned* /kənˈsɜːnd/

2. The word stress usually falls on the first syllable in two-syllable nouns (and adjectives), and on the second syllable in two-syllable verbs.

4.3   This exercise gives more practice in recognizing word stress and understanding its effects on pronunciation. There is no model version of this task on the recording, but you may like to model the pronunciation yourself. If you do, make sure you pronounce the words in the right-hand column with /ə/ as the initial vowel sound.

Answers (see Appendix 2a, page 26):

Oo	oO
access (n)	account (n)
aspect (n)	adapt (v)
contact (v/n)	assist (v)
context (n)	assume (v)
process (n)	connect (v)
product (n)	consist (v)
promise (v/n)	consume (v)
	control (v/n)
	produce (v)
	protect (v)
	provide (v)

a. See labels in the table above.

b. The word stress generally falls on the first syllable in two-syllable nouns (and adjectives), and on the second syllable in two-syllable verbs (of course, there are exceptions: *contact* and *control*, for example, both have the same noun and verb forms, and do not follow these word-stress patterns).
It is worth chorally drilling the words in the table. Check that students understand that in all the words in the right-hand column the vowel sound is /ə/, and insist that students pronounce it that way.

4.4 ▶ **CD1: 12** You may decide to drop exercises labelled *Easy* or *More demanding*; see page 9 for more information.

EASY

Answers:

Security is an important <u>aspect</u> of using a computer that many people do not pay much attention to. If you buy a laptop or personal computer, you will probably want to <u>connect</u> to the Internet. If so, it is important that you install security software which will protect it from attack by viruses or spyware. Now there is a wide range of <u>products</u> available on the market which are relatively cheap and which <u>provide</u> a variety of different features. For example, in addition to checking their computer for viruses, parents can use the software to <u>control</u> which websites their children can <u>access</u>. You should not <u>assume</u>, however, that you are 100% safe if you are using such security software. You should make sure that you have backup copies of your work, and you should be very careful about keeping important information, such as bank <u>account</u> details, on your computer.

4.5 ▶ **CD1: 13** Before students start listening, point out that although these are not words from the previous exercise, they follow the same word stress/pronunciation pattern.

MORE DEMANDING

Answers:

Because of planning restrictions, the large UK supermarket chains are looking to expand their businesses and increase <u>profits</u> by opening smaller 'convenience stores'. Organizations representing small, independent shops <u>protest</u> that they now face unfair competition from the large chains. And they <u>accuse</u> the large chains of a number of practices that make it difficult for them to compete. Firstly, it is <u>alleged</u> that below-cost pricing is used by large supermarkets to force smaller, local shops out of business. Secondly, the large chains often buy up land which is not immediately used, and this prevents smaller local businesses from entering the market.

There is also some <u>concern</u> that the large chains are treating their suppliers unfairly. Farmers claim that they are being paid less for their products, and are reluctant to complain for fear of losing key <u>contracts</u>. However, supermarkets argue that the <u>consumer</u> is the best regulator of the market.

Extension activity

Students label the answers according to what part of speech they are.

4.6　Follow the same procedure and patterns as for Ex 4.3. If you model the pronunciation of these words, try to pronounce the words in the right-hand column with /ə/ as the initial vowel sound.

Note: Some native speakers may pronounce the initial unstressed vowel spelt 'e' (*emerge*, *exceed*, *event*) as /e/.

Answers (see Appendix 2b, page 27):

Oo	oO
decent	decide
dentist	decline
equal	defend
even	delay
expert	effect
reckon	emerge
reptile	extinct
rescue	reflect
	rely
	report

4.7　▶ **CD1: 14** You could ask students here which words *do not* follow the patterns discussed in Ex 4.3. (*reckon*, *rescue*, *effect*, *extinct*, *report* (*n*)).

EASY

Equal and *reckon* are verbs, but have the stress on the first syllable; *event* is a noun, but has the word stress on the second syllable – many students get the word stress wrong on *event*; this may be because they are overgeneralizing.

Answers:

Wildlife <u>experts</u> predict that numbers of polar bears will <u>decline</u> by at least 50% over the next 50 years because of global warming. Polar bears <u>rely</u> on sea ice to catch seals for food, and it has <u>emerged</u> that ice floes in the Arctic are disappearing at an alarming rate. Now scientists <u>report</u> that the animals are already beginning to suffer the <u>effects</u> of climate change in some parts of Canada, and if there is any further <u>delay</u> in tackling this problem, polar bears may be <u>extinct</u> by the end of the century.

Extension activity
Students label the answers according to what part of speech they are.

4.8   ▶ **CD1: 15** Follow the same procedure as for Ex 4.7.

**MORE
DEMANDING**

Answers:
Scientists are now able to monitor river levels using information from satellites by using a computer program <u>devised</u> by researchers at De Montfort University in Leicester. Satellites have been able to measure the height of the sea by timing how long it takes to <u>receive</u> a beam bounced back off waves. But, until now, interference from objects on the banks of rivers has made it impossible to measure river levels.

However, the new programme, which is based on data collected over the last <u>decade</u>, is specially <u>designed</u> to filter out this interference. This new technology will be particularly useful in monitoring river levels in <u>remote</u> areas. It will, for example, enable scientists to <u>examine</u> river-level patterns over the <u>entire</u> Amazon River basin, contributing towards our understanding of climate change.

Extension activity
Students label the parts of speech for the answers.

Exercises 4.4, 4.5, 4.7 and 4.8 could be varied by students reading the transcript to each other in pairs.

Unit summary

1   This should be quite easy, but it is useful to discuss the language that might distract the students once they have completed the activity.

Answers:
a.   Why Britain is not part of the monetary union.
b.   Low-paid employment within the public sector.
c.   Crime that is drug-related.

Extension activity
Students could write their own mini introductions to topics which interest them and insert the distraction language. This will enable you to see if they fully understand the focus of Unit 2.

2   **Answers:**
a. scope   b. theory   c. content   d. research
e. background   f. approaches   g. previous   h. interest

Extension activity
For higher-level groups, students could make up their own lectures using the functions from Unit 2.

Oo	oO
access (n)	account (n)
aspect (n)	adapt (v)
contact (v/n)	assist (v)
context (n)	assume (v)
process (n)	connect (v)
product (n)	consist (v)
promise (v/n)	consume (v)
	control (v/n)
	produce (v)
	protect (v)
	provide (v)

PHOTOCOPIABLE

Appendix 2b

Oo	oO
decent	decide
dentist	decline
equal	defend
even	delay
expert	effect
reckon	emerge
reptile	extinct
rescue	reflect
	rely
	report

PHOTOCOPIABLE

3   Identifying key ideas in lectures

In this unit students will:

- practise identifying the key points a lecturer wants to make
- distinguish key points from examples
- use their understanding of examples to deduce key points
- develop their understanding of relationships between ideas
- learn patterns of pronunciation and word stress in word families

Task 1   Thinking about key ideas

The aim of this task is to generate ideas on the subject of the unit.

1.1   By this stage, students should have few problems coming up with answers to these questions. However, with weaker groups, you may want to provide suggestions for them to agree/disagree with.

Answers:

1. It is important to recognize and note down key ideas because this allows the listener to follow the main thread of the argument. If students can't distinguish between the key ideas and digressions and supporting detail, for example, they may find listening confusing and misleading.

2. Examples are used to make key ideas clearer, but can also be used to discredit other theories or approaches.

Task 2   Identifying key points in a lecture

The aim of Tasks 2–4 is that students should develop their ability to select key points from a lecture.

In Tasks 2, 3 and 4 students listen to a lecture on franchising. The lecture is divided into three parts, and each part is divided into two or three sections. After students have listened to each part, they listen again to the part divided into sections. The listening is structured as follows:

Task/Exercise	Part/Section
2.2	All of Part 1
2.3	Part 1, Section 1
2.4	Part 1, Section 2
2.5	Part 1, Section 3
3.2	All of Part 2
3.4	Part 2, Section 1
3.5	Part 2, Section 2
3.6	Part 2, Section 3
4.1	All of Part 3
4.2	Part 3, Section 1

4.3	Part 3, Section 2
4.4	Part 3, Section 3

This sequence of tasks requires students to make quite a detailed analysis of certain discourse features, and it can mean that they lose the thread of the overall argument. If you have a strong class or are under time pressure, you may prefer to do just Exercises 2.1, 2.2, 3.2 and 4.1.

2.1   **Note:** Franchising is a way of doing business, in which people can buy an enterprise and benefit from an established image or brand. The Body Shop is an example of a franchise operation: people buy the right to open an outlet of The Body Shop, they have to run the outlet according to guidelines set by The Body Shop organization (the franchisor), and the profits or losses from the outlet go to the buyer of the franchise (the franchisee). Here the definition of franchising is given by the lecturer.

Answers:

1. 'Business format franchising is the granting of a licence by one person (the franchisor) to another (the franchisee), which entitles the franchisee to trade under the trademark or trade name of the franchisor and to make use of an entire package, comprising all the elements necessary to establish a previously untrained person in the business, and to run it with continual assistance on a predetermined basis.' *British Franchising Association website*

2. McDonalds, Dunkin' Donuts, Kumon Education and Printfast are examples of franchise businesses.

2.2   ▶ **CD1: 16** The aim of this exercise is to encourage students to see a logical organizational structure to this first part of the lecture. In addition, to do the task they will also need to be able to distinguish supporting detail from the main point of each section. Give students time to read through the list before they listen.

Answers:

The three sections of Part 1 in the correct order are:

1. one reason for setting up a franchise business

2. a definition of franchising

3. how franchising works

2.3   ▶ **CD1: 17** Check that students understand the vocabulary in the box and the questions. Use concept-check questions with lower levels and ask higher-level students to reformulate questions to check understanding.

Answers:

1. You may need:
   - large amounts of capital
   - to reorganize your business
   - to bring new skills into the management team

2. A small chain of hairdressing salons.

3. You have to invest a lot of money and you may not be able to exert as much personal control over the running of the business as you have been used to.

4. Key point: Franchising your business can minimize the risks involved in its expansion.

2.4 ▶ **CD1: 18** Check students understand the questions, particularly 2, where they have to understand that this is a hypothetical situation aimed at checking they understand the *franchisor/franchisee* roles.

Answers:

1. Business format franchising.

2. • McDonald's is the franchisor.
   • Bill Jones is the (prospective) franchisee.

3. The licence entitles the franchisee to:
   • trade under the trademark/trade name of the franchisor
   • make use of a package (of support from the franchisor)

4. The package would include:
   • training
   • consultancy arrangements
   • (possibly) supplies
   • marketing (on a national scale)

2.5 ▶ **CD1: 19** Check students understand the questions.

Answers:

1. Signage and materials (necessary to maintain a uniform brand).

2. An initial fee (paid at the beginning of the business arrangement) and an ongoing management service fee.

3. The initial fee is a one-off payment. The management service fee is paid regularly, and related to the volume of business (possibly as a percentage of turnover, or a mark-up on supplies provided by franchisor).

4. The key point of this section is to show how each party benefits.

Task 3	Distinguishing key points from examples

The aim of Task 3 is that students should recognize the difference between key points and examples.

3.1 Do this exercise in pairs or as a whole class and elicit the ideas from students to put on the board.

It can be inferred here that the lecturer may go on to talk about factors you need to consider when franchising your business and, possibly, advantages and disadvantages of franchising.

3.2 ▶ **CD1: 20** Students may note down slightly different main points. The sample notes on page 32 show the authors' perception of the main points. For lower-level students, rather than taking their own notes, the sample notes handout on page 36 can be adapted as scaffolding; delete some key words which the students complete while listening. The underlined words are key words; these are the words you should delete if adapting the task for lower-level students.

Sample notes (see Appendix 3a, page 36):

<u>Franchising your business</u>: Issues to consider:

- Need <u>stable, long-term</u> market for product/service
- <u>Wide margin</u> costs – income = profit for franchisor and franchisee
- Support/training for franchisee > detailed <u>operating manual</u>
- Franchisee needs to develop skills to run business <u>quickly</u>

3.3   You should make it clear that speakers do not always use signposting language systematically. After *Firstly*, one might expect to hear *Secondly*, *Thirdly*, etc., but this does not always happen.

Answers:

In addition to *Firstly*, the students should be able to identify:

- *In addition*
- *The important point here is*

You may wish to use the transcript to identify other useful language at lower and higher levels. Examples could be: *this*, *so*, *well*, *however*, etc.

3.4   ▶ **CD1: 21** Check students understand the questions.

Answers:

1. The two <u>reasons</u> are:
   - you need substantial investment to set up a franchise operation
   - you need an established market with potential for long-term growth to attract franchisees

   The two <u>examples</u> are:
   - hairdressing salons
   - a new kind of children's toy

2. The two examples illustrate the point about the need for a 'relatively stable, long-term market'; the first a positive example, and the second a negative example, of products/ services which meet this criterion.

When note-taking, students need to make instant decisions about whether or not to note down examples like this. If they make the key points clearer or more memorable, they may be worth noting down.

3.5   ▶ **CD1: 22** Check students understand the questions.

Answers:

1. Buying in bulk enables franchisees and franchisors to keep their costs down.

2. This is an example of one way in which you can ensure that there is a wide margin between costs and income.

3. In addition – and this is fairly obvious – <u>you will need a fairly wide margin between cost and income</u>. Remember that the gross margin needs to provide a return on the investment to both the franchisor and the franchisee. <u>So you will need to keep costs low and prices as high as the market will bear</u>. One advantage of a franchise operation is that supplies can be bought in bulk across the whole franchise, which will help to keep costs down. But you can see that <u>franchising would be unsuitable in a market where the margin between cost and income is very narrow</u>.

3.6   ▶ **CD1: 23** Check students understand the questions.

Answers:

1. Support, training and an operating manual.

2. These will be required when setting up the franchise and possibly on a regular, ongoing basis.

3. Franchisees in the restaurant business are likely to already have experience in the restaurant industry or a similar field (because they need to get the franchise up and running very quickly).

4. The key point is that the franchisee needs to be able to develop the skills needed to operate the franchise *quickly*. This point is clearly signposted: *The important point here is …*

Task 4	Signposting and highlighting key points

The aim of this task is to show students how lecturers use signposting language and stress/pauses to highlight key points.

4.1   ▶ **CD1: 24** Students may not take notes as detailed as these. One approach to take may be to elicit from students the notes they have made, write them up on the board, and then add to them, as you play the different sections in Part 3 one by one.

Sample notes (see Appendix 3a, page 36):

Franchising your business: Issues to consider (cont.)**:**

- Is business transferable? From small localized area to larger market?
- importance of protecting brand
- quality standards > operating manual + written agreement
- care selecting + monitoring franchisees; should have same business values
- regular visits + training

4.2   ▶ **CD1: 25** The missing words in this task are key words which the lecturer stresses. It may also be worth playing this section again to draw students' attention to the way the lecturer pauses slightly after each key point.

Answers:

One further issue you may need to consider is whether the business is <u>transferable</u> to another geographical area. If you have developed your business serving one particular part of the country and you want to set up a franchise network covering a <u>much larger area</u> – the whole country, for example – another thing you will have to consider is whether there is a <u>similar market</u> for your product or service in different regions. It may be, for example, that competition in other parts of the country may be so <u>strong</u> that it is difficult for franchisees to <u>survive</u>, or that for localized <u>socioeconomic</u> or <u>cultural</u> reasons the business may not be as profitable.

4.3 ▶ **CD1: 26** Students may perceive that other words are stressed; this is because there seems to be a kind of hierarchy of sentence stress, rather than a clear stressed/unstressed distinction between words.

Answers: (signposting language is <u>underlined</u>; key words and phrases stressed by the lecturer are highlighted) (see Appendix 3b, page 37)

<u>Finally,</u> when you are setting up a franchise network, you will need to bear in mind that you will be losing direct control of the way your brand is perceived by the customer, so <u>this</u> brings me to my last point, which is to emphasize the importance of protecting your brand. I am sure you are all aware that it often takes a long time to establish a distinctive brand with a valuable reputation, but that this reputation can be damaged comparatively quickly, if, for example, quality standards are not consistently applied. The detailed operating manual that I referred to earlier will play a role in maintaining the brand but, <u>just as important,</u> you need to take care selecting franchisees and monitoring their operations. <u>In addition to</u> checking that franchisees have the relevant skills and experience to run a successful business, <u>you also need to</u> ensure that they share the same business values as you, that they accept the importance of maintaining the brand and that they are clear about what they can or can't change about the way the business is run – so people who are very individualistic will probably not make good franchisees.

4.4 ▶ **CD1: 27** Point out that some function words (e.g., auxiliary verbs, articles) can be omitted in notes if the meaning remains clear to the student. Inessential function words are in brackets in these notes.

Sample notes (see Appendix 3b, page 37):

Protecting the brand

1. *Written agreement should specify <u>what performance and quality standards (are) expected.</u>*

2. *Initial training – to ensure staff <u>have skills to achieve these standards.</u>*

3. *Regular visits – to ensure <u>standards (are being) applied consistently and uniformly.</u>*

4. *Ongoing training – to deal with <u>issues (that are) uncovered in visits.</u>*

5. *Protecting the brand is in the interests of <u>both franchisor + franchisee.</u>*

The final question can be done as a whole class, group or pair discussion.

Extension activity

With higher-level students you might want to include a summary writing activity as a way of consolidating the lecture.

Task 5	Microskills: Word families (1)

This task focuses on word stress patterns and differences in pronunciation between words in word families. Students may fail to recognize a word because the stress may be on a different syllable from another word in the same word family which they are familiar with.

5.1 If necessary, model the pronunciation of the words in the table. Ensure that you drill students on each word.

Answers:

Noun	Verb	Adjective
product, production, productivity	produce	productive
definition	define	definite, definitive
economy, economics, economist	economize	economic, economical

5.2   Give students some time to study the words and the pronunciation changes. They can work individually or in pairs. Conduct feedback highlighting pronunciation changes and use phonemic symbols where necessary.

5.3   ▶ **CD1: 28** You could discuss the general meanings of some of these prefixes and elicit examples of other words that begin with them.

Answers:

1. All trade unions were declared illegal by the government.

2. This is one example of a mismatch between the individual's goals and those of the organization.

3. They found no significant correlation between class size and levels of achievement.

4. Real estate transactions rose by 30% last month.

5. Prices are determined through the interaction of supply and demand.

6. These animals exhibited abnormal behaviour compared to the control group.

5.4   ▶ **CD1: 29** In this exercise, students have to decide where the word boundaries are (e.g., ... in direct ... or ... indirect ...?) They may have difficulty with this, so do question 1 as an example.

Answers:

1. We had to get the photos enlarged because the detail was not very clear on the original ones.

2. Many doctors work long, irregular hours, which puts them under a lot of stress.

3. Crime prevention is an important aspect of the police's work, but it is often difficult to assess its effectiveness.

4. Doctors have noticed an increase in eating disorders, such as bulimia and anorexia, not just among young women but, surprisingly, among young men.

5. These plants should be grown in partial shade, rather than in direct sunlight.

6. Researchers have found that inexperienced drivers are much more likely to be involved in traffic accidents.

Elicit the answers from students, write them on the board and drill the pronunciation.

5.5 ▶ **CD1: 30** This exercise is more demanding because students have to identify the word boundaries. Again, do question 1 as an example with the whole class.

Answers:

1. a. Children need a <u>secure</u> environment in which to grow up.
   b. Many immigrants are only able to find <u>low-paid, insecure jobs</u>.
   c. The money was invested in <u>securities</u> and property.

2. a. Achievement levels <u>vary</u> considerably from school to school in the city.
   b. Some economists believe that interest rates can be predicted by examining <u>key economic variables.</u>
   c. In the Eden Project they have managed to create <u>a wide variety of</u> habitats.
   d. There is <u>significant variation in access</u> to health care in different parts of the country.

3. a. How are we going to <u>solve</u> this problem?
   b. You need to <u>dissolve the pesticide</u> in water before applying it to the crop.
   c. There appears to be <u>insoluble conflict</u> between the two countries, despite years of peace negotiations.

4. a. A mass spectrometer was used to <u>analyze</u> the gases.
   b. <u>Further analysis</u> of the data is needed to confirm these initial findings.
   c. The course is designed to help students to develop <u>their analytical skills</u>.

5. a. The results <u>indicate</u> that the virus mutates more rapidly than was first believed.
   b. All the <u>main economic indicators</u> suggest that the economy is recovering.
   c. The strike was <u>indicative of</u> the level of the workers' frustration.

6. a. Chomsky was a fierce <u>critic</u> of Bush Senior's foreign policy.
   b. There was <u>some criticism of</u> the way the election had been administered.
   c. The negotiations <u>were critical to the</u> establishment of peace in the area.

You may want to spend some time looking at the meanings and uses of some of these words, e.g., the difference between *variation* and *variety*, or the fact that *critical* in this context has a different meaning from *critic* and *criticism*.

Unit 7 has more work on word families.

Unit summary

This could be done in pairs or as a class quiz.

Answers:

1. All are true except points b and f.

2. When students have ticked the response that is correct for them, make sure you record which students still require further practice and give them some follow-up work for homework.

3. Examples of signposting language are:
   firstly, another thing is, one further issue, for example, in addition, finally, the important point here, one advantage is, so, remember

Sample notes:

Franchising your business: Issues to consider:

- Need _stable_, _long-term_ market for product/service
- _Wide margin_ costs – income = profit for franchisor and franchisee
- Support/training for franchisee > detailed _operating manual_
- Franchisee needs to develop skills to run business _quickly_

Sample notes:

Franchising your business: Issues to consider (cont.):

- Is business transferable? From small localized area to larger market?
- importance of protecting brand
- quality standards > operating manual + written agreement
- care selecting + monitoring franchisees; should have same business values
- regular visits + training

PHOTOCOPIABLE

Appendix 3b

Answers:

(Signposting language is <u>underlined</u>. Key words and phrases stressed by the lecturer are highlighted.)

<u>Finally</u>, when you are setting up a franchise network, you will need to bear in mind that you will be losing direct control of the way your brand is perceived by the customer, so <u>this brings me to my last point</u>, which is to emphasize the importance of protecting your brand. I am sure you are all aware that it often takes a long time to establish a distinctive brand with a valuable reputation, but that this reputation can be damaged comparatively quickly, if, for example, quality standards are not consistently applied. The detailed operating manual that I referred to earlier will play a role in maintaining the brand but, <u>just as important</u>, you need to take care selecting franchisees and monitoring their operations. <u>In addition to</u> checking that franchisees have the relevant skills and experience to run a successful business, <u>you also need to</u> ensure that they share the same business values as you, that they accept the importance of maintaining the brand and that they are clear about what they can or can't change about the way the business is run – so people who are very individualistic will probably not make good franchisees.

<u>Protecting the brand</u>

1. Written agreement should specify <u>what performance and quality standards (are) expected.</u>

2. Initial training – to ensure staff <u>have skills to achieve these standards.</u>

3. Regular visits – to ensure <u>standards (are being) applied consistently and uniformly.</u>

4. Ongoing training – to deal with <u>issues (that are) uncovered in visits.</u>

5. Protecting the brand is in the interests of <u>both franchisor + franchisee.</u>

PHOTOCOPIABLE

4   Note-taking: Part 1

In this unit students will:

- discuss the reasons for taking notes in a lecture
- learn the principles of effective note-taking
- practise taking notes from lectures

Task 1   Reasons for taking notes

The focus of this task is to orient students to the topic and for the teacher to find out how familiar students are with note-taking and why it is important. You may want to show students some notes you have taken as an example.

1.1

1. Students should come up with some of the following ideas.
    - Lectures often provide an overview of a particular area of study, and as such may provide a starting point from which students work on assignments requiring more detailed study. So students may need to use notes as reference points for more independent study.
    - For some students, the process of making notes helps them to concentrate on the content and organization of the lecture. If they don't take notes, their mind may drift off.
    - It is unlikely that students will understand everything they hear. Their notes should therefore include reminders of questions or issues they want to follow up, whether with other students or with the lecturer.
    - It may be that students will be tested on the content of lectures, and therefore need them to revise from.

2. **Possible answers:**
    - Read through notes within 24 hours of a lecture to check that they make sense.
    - Review notes again one or two weeks later.
    - Form study groups to review notes together immediately after lectures (this is a useful cooperative strategy).
    - Rewrite notes within 24 hours of a lecture (this process helps students to consolidate their understanding and also to reorganize notes in a way that is clearer and easier to revise from).

3. Lecture notes are generally personal and so the volume and specific focus of notes will vary from one student to another.

4. Students should be selective, because no one has time to write everything down. In general, students should write down the key ideas, and any examples they need to make sense of the key ideas. Many lecturers also use the introductory stages of lectures for 'course management' purposes, e.g., they remind students of deadlines for assignments or tell them of changes to the timetable, and students may need to note down such information.
    Students should not note down all the repetitions of ideas, digressions and multiple examples that characterize many lectures. A student who is already very familiar with the content of a lecture is likely to take fewer notes than one who is less familiar – it is not necessary to note down what you know already – that said, students who believe they are already very familiar with the content of the lecture would be foolish not to take any notes at all. The process of taking notes focuses the mind and keeps a student alert to any 'new' content.

Task 2   Principles of note-taking

The aim of this task is to familiarize students with the principles of note-taking and give them practice in the mechanics of note-taking.

2.1   These pre-listening questions could be discussed in pairs or as a whole class. The exercise is designed to encourage students to apply their background knowledge to predicting the content of the lecture, so do not prompt them too much.

You may wish to drop or adapt this pre-listening exercise, depending on the students' background knowledge, and whether or not they are studying in the UK. You might instead ask students about the traffic situation in their own countries.

Possible answers:
Students might make some of the following points:

1. Reasons why there are so many cars on the roads:
   - Britain is a relatively affluent, developed country, so people can afford cars.
   - Small island with a high population density (especially in the south-east).

2. Problems:
   - traffic jams
   - air pollution
   - health problems

3. Ways of reducing the amount of traffic:
   - increasing tax on petrol
   - improving public transport
   - encouraging people to share cars
   - banning cars from certain roads at certain times

2.2   ▶ **CD1: 31** You may want to get students to highlight the key points as they read, using the techniques from Unit 3.

2.3   **Possible answers:**
1. These are the key points.
2. The notes are sufficiently detailed.
3. Would the student realize, for example, that it is the time wasted in traffic jams that leads to loss of productivity for commuters?
4. a. layout (bullet points)
   b. abbreviations and symbols

2.4   Discuss the annotated text with students. You may want students to annotate the rest of the text in Ex 2.2 in the same way.

2.5   ▶ **CD1: 32–CD1: 35** Having talked about some of the problems, one would expect the lecturer to go on to discuss solutions to the problem.

Make sure you model the pronunciation of the vocabulary in Parts 2–5 and ask students to explain the meanings before listening.

These parts of the lecture follow on from Part 1. Check that students understand the key vocabulary, and then remind them that they only need to write down the key ideas.

Depending on how strong your class is, you could either check the notes after each part of the lecture, or you could play all four parts, possibly pausing between each one to allow students to compare notes, and then check all three parts.

Sample notes (see Appendix 4a, page 44):

Part 2

Not <u>one</u> solution,

- e.g., road-building not solution, bec. > more traffic
- but <u>range</u> of measures needed (ITP)
- transport = political issue

Part 3

1997 Public consult. on ITP (rail, road, air, etc.)

- One issue: encourage drivers to use publ. transp? This is not enough, bec. drs. will still prefer to use cars.

Part 4

Not one solution, but package, e.g.,

- car-sharing; lanes for use by cars with more than one person
- congestion charging; charging cars to enter some zones. Reduces no. of cars + income can be invested in pub. transp.

Part 5

Schemes put pressure on drs.

- coalition wants to = dev rail network – connect N/S Engl. + new airport

Focus students' attention on the *Sound advice* section. If you use the suggested answers above, they should illustrate the *selective, brief, clear* principles. To test whether the notes are effective, a week later you could project the notes above on a visual aid and see if students can reconstruct the ideas from them.

You may also want to use the transcript as part of feedback. Ask students to highlight the areas of the transcript where the notes are taken from and notice the proportion of text which has not been recorded. This can help increase students' confidence that they do not need to understand and write down every word.

Task 3	Note-taking practice

The aim of this task is to guide students through the note-taking process with an authentic lecture. The script for this listening exercise comes from an authentic lecture and is fairly demanding. There is a certain amount of unfamiliar (but unimportant) vocabulary that students may be distracted by, e.g., *swashbuckling*.

3.1 Students should be able to come up with answers to the pre-listening questions, and thereby predict the content of the listening texts. Elicit responses from students, but do not tell them the correct answers.

Answers:

Answers depend on students.

Model the pronunciation and check meaning of the vocabulary in the boxes for Ex 3.2 and 3.3.

3.2   ▶ **CD1: 36** Students listen and complete the notes.

Note: *Market liberalism* refers to opening up markets to competition by removing regulation. *Swashbuckling* usually refers to a brave, adventurous approach to warfare, and in this context refers to a similar approach to business competition.

Sample notes (see Appendix 4b, page 45):

Part 1

Interpreting East Asian economic miracle.
- *Dispute about influence of market liberalism*
- *e.g., China – highly controlled economy*
- *Japan, South Korea – not totally free market*
- *Singapore, HK – free market*
- *State intervention or free market > miracle?*

3.3   ▶ **CD1: 37**

Part 2

Everyone agreed about one element –
- *EA countries invested in people (health care, ed. + training)*
- *Low labour rates + high skills*

For Exercises 3.2 and 3.3 you may need to give students some scaffolding to help them note the correct points. Options include adapting the sample notes above or pre-teaching some of the lexis from the listening. You need to ensure that your students are able to note down some key information to build their confidence.

After giving feedback on students' note-taking, you may want to allow students to listen to the lecture again and read the transcript, especially with lower-level students.

Task 4	Microskills: Sentence stress

This task focuses on the apparent effect of sentence stress in 'compressing sounds' between the main stressed syllables, leading to weak forms, linking, elision and assimilation.

4.1   ▶ **CD1: 38** Play the short section from the previous extract and check that students can hear that certain syllables are stressed. Check that they understand that key content words tend to receive the stress.

Focus on *a lot of people* and elicit (or show them) that:
- *lot* is pronounced /lɒt/ in this context, and *of* is pronounced /əv/
- in speech, the four words are run together so that they sound like a single word

4.2   ▶ **CD1: 39** The sentences give more examples of weak forms and linking. It is worth pointing out that effective listeners may not actually 'hear' these weak forms, and instead construct the meaning on the basis of their language knowledge. So, most native speakers would be able to 'fill in' the first and third gaps quite easily without actually listening. The implication here is that learners have to develop an awareness of the syntactic patterns of spoken English to improve their listening skills. Studying the transcripts and focusing on unfamiliar structures or patterns may help.

Answers:

- The Japanese <u>have</u> never run <u>a</u> purely free-market economy. Neither <u>have</u> the Koreans.

Model the answer and drill students to raise their awareness of the weak forms. You may want to show students more examples of connected speech and weak forms and do a lot more pronunciation work in class.

4.3   ▶ **CD1: 40** Check that students understand the context for this extract before you play it. Pauses have been put between the short sections to give students time to fill in the gaps.

Answers (see Appendix 4c, page 46):

You need to pre-test the questionnaire. This is really important. Those of you, some of you, will be doing this for, you know, your dissertation. Some of you, I know, <u>are collecting primary data</u>. You need to pre-test the thing, because you're the researcher. You're very <u>close to the subject.</u> You know what you're talking about, but you've got to check that other people do as well. And if you want a statistically valid sample of a hundred people or two hundred people, <u>then you've got to make sure that</u> you're collecting the data properly. And it's here that these <u>pre-tests, or pilots</u>, they're going to tell you whether it's going to work or not.

So make sure that you do pilots and, you know, this can be, sort of, <u>half a dozen</u> different people that you question. I mean, you'll soon find out whether you've got any potential … or any doubts about the length of the questionnaire, <u>or the style of particular questions</u>, or whether the sort of questions that you're asking are valid. You'll soon find out from that. So, piloting or pre-testing is really important.

It is worth spending some time on this excerpt with students, because it illustrates a number of features of a conversational lecturing style:

- The language can be relatively informal (e.g., *You need to pre-test* **the thing**.)
- There is a lot more coordination (*and … and … so … and …*) than in written English.
- There are fillers (*sort of … you know …*).
- There are false starts (*Those of you, some of you, will be doing this for …*).

4.4   **Answers:**

1. The primary stressed syllables are marked with '.
   - are col'lecting 'primary 'data
   - 'close to the 'subject
   - you've 'got to make 'sure that
   - 'pre-tests, or 'pilots
   - half a 'dozen
   - or the 'style of particular 'questions

2. Check that students realize that the function words are generally unstressed, and often the vowel sound is /ə/.

Unit summary

This activity could be done in pairs or as a class quiz.

1. **Answers:**
   a. be selective about what you write down
   b. keep notes brief
   c. you
   d. must write down key words related to the topic

   e. sometimes use abbreviations to save time
   f. make sure that the way points relate to one another is clear

2. Students can discuss the questions in pairs or groups. They should make a list of ways to improve their note-taking and their progress can be discussed later in the course.

3. **Answers:**
    a. imp<u>or</u>tant, eff<u>ec</u>tively, <u>lec</u>ture
    b. The stressed syllables will depend on how the speaker delivers the sentence, particularly on what he/she wishes to emphasize; prepositions and articles (e.g., *for*, *to*, *a*) are not usually stressed.
    c. They help identify what is important to the speaker.

Extension activity
Show students how the meaning changes when the stress is put on different words. You can then discuss when and why the speaker would want to change the stress pattern.

Sample notes:

Part 2

Not <u>one</u> solution,

- e.g., road–building not solution, bec. > more traffic
- but <u>range</u> of measures needed (ITP)
- transport = political issue

Part 3

1997 Public consult. on ITP (rail, road, air, etc.)

- One issue: encourage drivers to use publ. transp? This is not enough, bec. drs. will still prefer to use cars.

Part 4

Not one solution, but package, e.g.,

- car–sharing; lanes for use by cars with more than one person
- congestion charging; charging cars to enter some zones. Reduces no. of cars + income can be invested in pub. transp.

Part 5

Schemes put pressure on drs.

- coalition wants to = dev rail network – connect N/S Engl. + new airport

PHOTOCOPIABLE

Appendix 4b

Sample notes:

Part 1

Interpreting East Asian economic miracle.
- Dispute about influence of market liberalism
- e.g., China – highly controlled economy
- Japan, South Korea – not totally free market
- Singapore, HK – free market
- State intervention or free market > miracle?

Part 2

Everyone agreed about one element –
- EA countries invested in people (health care, ed. + training)
- Low labour rates + high skills

PHOTOCOPIABLE

Answers:

You need to pre-test the questionnaire. This is really important. Those of you, some of you, will be doing this for, you know, your dissertation. Some of you, I know, <u>are collecting primary data</u>. You need to pre-test the thing, because you're the researcher. You're very <u>close to the subject</u>. You know what you're talking about, but you've got to check that other people do as well. And if you want a statistically valid sample of a hundred people or two hundred people, <u>then you've got to make sure that</u> you're collecting the data properly. And it's here that these <u>pre-tests, or pilots,</u> they're going to tell you whether it's going to work or not.

So make sure that you do pilots and, you know, this can be, sort of, <u>half a dozen</u> different people that you question. I mean, you'll soon find out whether you've got any potential … or any doubts about the length of the questionnaire, <u>or the style of particular questions,</u> or whether the sort of questions that you're asking are valid. You'll soon find out from that. So piloting or pre-testing is really important.

PHOTOCOPIABLE

Note-taking: Part 2

In this unit students will:

- learn how to use abbreviations and symbols to save time when note-taking
- discuss the advantages and disadvantages of two ways of taking notes
- practise note-taking from lectures

This unit consolidates and extends work done on note-taking in the previous unit. It looks at the use of abbreviations and symbols in taking notes, and the relative merits of linear and 'mind-map' formats for notes. The microskills section takes a more detailed look at the linking of words in natural speech and the problems this presents for listeners.

| Task 1 | Returning to your notes |

The aim of this task is to show students how they can expand their notes back out to full sentences.

1.1   You need to provide students with a copy of notes that have been made from a lecture or lecture extract that students have listened to recently. You can either use the notes below (also available on page 54 as a photocopiable handout) from the lecture on UK transport problems in the previous unit, or if you prefer, use notes taken from another lecture the students have listened to. If you opt for the latter, please ensure that you have used some abbreviations and symbols in your notes.

You will probably need to show students what you expect of them by expanding the first few notes, e.g., *Roads in the UK are very overcrowded and this has had a number of effects. Firstly, there are economic effects …*

It is also worth reminding students of basic S+V+O sentence structure and linking ideas together with cohesive devices.

Sample notes (see Appendix 5a, page 54):

Integrated Transport Policy (ITP)

UK roads overcrowded → effects

- economic; ↘ prod.vity
- environmental; poll., glob. warming
- health probs.; lung, heart disease

Not one solution,

- e.g., road–building not solution, bec. → more traffic
- but range of measures needed (ITP)
- transport = political issue

1997 Public consult. on ITP

- One issue: encourage drivers to use publ. transp?
- Not enough, bec. drs. will still prefer to use cars.

Not one solution, but package, e.g.:

- car–sharing; lanes for use by cars with more than 1 person
- congestion charging; charging cars to enter some zones. Reduces no. of cars + income can be invested in publ. transp.

Schemes put pressure on drs.

■ *coalition wants to dev rail network – connect N/S Engl. + new airport*

Note: These notes have been slightly amended from the version in the previous unit.

Task 2	**Using abbreviations and symbols**

This task focuses on abbreviations and symbols in note-taking as a way of saving time.

2.1   If you used the notes provided in Task 1, students should come up with the following abbreviations and answers. You may want to do this exercise as a whole class and record their answers on the board.

Answers:

ITP	=	*Integrated Transport Policy*
→	=	lead to, result in
↘	=	decreased
prod.vity	=	productivity
poll.	=	pollution
glob. warming	=	global warming
health probs.	=	health problems
publ. transp.	=	public transport
bec.	=	because
drs.	=	drivers
no.	=	number
+	=	and/also/in addition
dev	=	develop

2.2   Often the abbreviations only make sense in context. Remind students that many abbreviations are personal, i.e., there are no rules about them.

You could give a few examples from the field of applied linguistics, e.g,:

Many gram. and pron. errors ← influence of L1.

(Many grammar and pronunciation errors are caused by the influence of a student's first language.)

Possible answers:

infl.	=	inflation
invest.	=	investment
recess.	=	recession
bus.	=	business
org.	=	organization
min.	=	minimum

2.3   **Answers (see Appendix 5b, page 55):**

Symbol	Meaning	Symbol	Meaning
↗	increase, rise, go up	≠	does not equal/is the opposite of
↘	fall, drop, decline, go down	€	euro
→	lead to, result in …	?	I don't understand this./I'm not sure.
←	caused by, result from …	!	This is surprising.
≥	is more than or equal to		

Ask students if they use any other symbols and record these on the board.

Task 3	Note-taking practice

This task gives students practice using abbreviations and symbols when listening.

3.1   ▶ **CD1: 41** Before this note-taking practice exercise, remind students to use abbreviations and symbols.

Sample notes (see Appendix 5c, page 56):
Extract 1

3 purposes of education (Littlewood, 1992):

   1   to pass on value, knowl. + cult.

   2   to prepare Ss as members of soc.

   3   humanistic; to develop indiv. to fulfil their potential

3.2   ▶ **CD1: 42** Check that students understand the key vocabulary before they listen. This is quite a demanding listening exercise, but there is a certain amount of repetition of ideas. If you think students are going to struggle, write a brief outline of the lecture on the board to help students follow the content.

Sample notes (see Appendix 5c, page 56):
Extract 2

early 70s econ. boom → infl. in world econ.

1971 US $ left gold standard > $ effectively devalued

(1970 US econ = 1/3 world econ.)

Exch. rates floated → major industr. economies' infl. rates ↗ to 10, 15, 20%

1971 UK infl. rate = 25%!!!

This task focuses on the relative merits of linear notes and mind maps. It does not deal with annotating a handout or PowerPoint outline, which you may want to refer to at some point.

4.1   Elicit from students what type of notes they normally use: linear or mind maps. If they are not familiar with the latter, demonstrate with a diagram on the board which refers back to a lecture they have heard during the course so far.

Ask students to read the descriptions of the lectures and discuss in pairs whether mind maps or linear notes would be more suitable in each case. Have a quick plenary feedback session. Encourage students to give reasons for their choices. There are no right or wrong answers here, although linear notes might seem more appropriate for 3.

4.2   **a.**   ▶ **CD1: 43** Before students listen, answer any queries they have about the vocabulary. Note the following information:

- In the UK, most drugs and medicines have to be prescribed by the doctor. That is to say, the doctor will examine the patient and decide what treatment is needed. The doctor then writes a *prescription* indicating what drugs the patient should take, when and how often. The patient then takes this prescription to the chemist, who sells her/him the drugs at a fixed price.

- *The British Heart Foundation* is a charity which conducts research into heart disease, and provides care and support to patients with heart conditions.

Before students listen, make sure they know which person in the pair is going to take notes in each style.

b.   When students have completed discussing the notes they have taken with their partner, encourage them to talk to other pairs and compare notes. Were there any differences in terms of content or style? Ask a few pairs which style they thought was more appropriate for this lecture. Ask them to give reasons. Open the discussion up and see if there is a consensus about the lecture.

Sample notes (see Appendix 5d, page 57):
Linear

Health in dev.ed world, esp. UK
- Life expectancy ↗, taking more drugs, controlling many illnesses BUT not avoiding getting sick
- UK life expectancy; deaths of men 35–74 ↘ 42% 1990–2000
  Reason: taking more drugs
  e.g., prescr. of drugs for heart disease ↗ X 4 in last 20 years
- Need to tackle <u>causes</u> of heart disease
  1 physical inactivity (people walking ↘, cycling ↘ but driving ↗)
  2 unhealthy diet → obesity, % of obese adults → X 2 in last 12 yrs
- cf Norway – deaths of men 35–74 ↘ 54% 1990–2000

Mind map

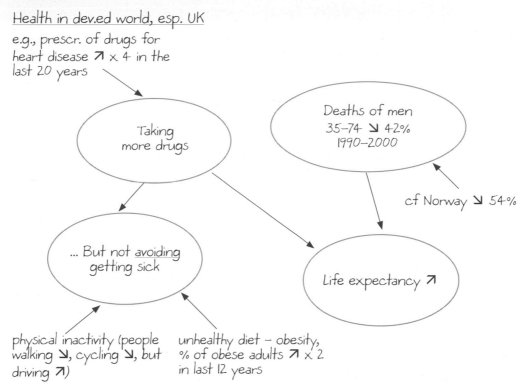

Health in dev.ed world, esp. UK

e.g., prescr. of drugs for heart disease ↗ x 4 in the last 20 years

Taking more drugs

Deaths of men 35–74 ↘ 42% 1990–2000

cf Norway ↘ 54%

... But not avoiding getting sick

Life expectancy ↗

physical inactivity (people walking ↘, cycling ↘, but driving ↗)

unhealthy diet – obesity, % of obese adults ↗ x 2 in last 12 years

4.3/ 4.4   Ask one or two pairs to report back on their discussion. The other pairs can listen and add any advantages or disadvantages that have not been mentioned.

Possible answers (see Appendix 5e, page 58):

	Advantages	Disadvantages
Linear notes	■ More familiar format ■ Easier to carry over to next page ■ Better for lectures arranged chronologically ■ Better for a lecture which contrasts different methods/ theories – can do linear notes but side by side	■ If you miss something out, it can be difficult to find a space in which to insert it
Mind maps	■ Visually appealing ■ Better for showing sense relationships ■ May be more suitable for lectures which lack clear organization ■ Easier to revise from ■ Easier to remember, especially for people with good visual memories	■ How do you link ideas if you have to carry over to a new page? ■ Ideas not always organized clearly

Task 5	Microskills: Word boundaries

This task focuses on linking between words and the problems this creates in identifying word boundaries and recognizing words.

5.1   ▶ **CD1: 44** These three sentences are on the recording, but you may prefer to read them out yourself.

1. The government has introduced <u>tax incentives</u> to encourage investment in this region.

2. For <u>tax purposes</u> these organizations are often regarded as charities.

3. A number of reforms to the <u>tax system</u> have been proposed.

In sentence 1 it may be difficult for the students to identify the word boundary and they may hear something like *tack sincentive*.

In sentence 3 there is only one /s/ sound in *tax system*, so they may hear *tack system*.

5.2   ▶ **CD1: 45** Have students read through the explanation and then play the recording or model the pronunciation yourself. If you just speak naturally, you should produce the features (there is more information about the intrusive /w/, /j/ or /r/ sounds in *EAS: Pronunciation*).

You might also point out that there is a certain amount of variation in pronunciation. For example, some British speakers use a glottal stop /ʔ/ instead of final /t/ whatever the context, while others pronounce /t/ in most contexts. For example, many speakers would pronounce *a short break* as /ə ʃɔːʔ breɪk/ and *went in the car* as /wenʔ ɪn ðə kɑː/.

5.3   ▶ **CD1: 46** If you think your students are able, ask them to mark up the sentences before you play them or say them yourself.

Possible answers:

1. they /j/ invested‿in property

2. a mixture /r/ of‿oil‿and residues

3. it's‿an‿open market

4. it's due /w/ on Friday morning

5. free /j/ admission‿on Sundays

6. it shows‿as‿a white mark

After feedback, drill students on the sentences.

5.4   ▶ **CD1: 47** Allow students time to read the text and clarify any words they do not understand. This exercise requires students to apply what they have learnt about listening to decode language. Some, but not all of the gaps include linked words.

It is interesting to note that the speaker pauses very frequently, so sometimes you don't get the linking you might expect. Students may also have problems recognizing weak forms of prepositions.

Answers (see Appendix 5f, page 59):

I'm going to go through the theory of real options, and then I'm going to show you how they can be used to <u>raise some money</u>, particularly on property assets. 'Real options' is a term which was coined ten or 15 years ago, when people began to realize that <u>net present value</u> isn't the only thing you should look at in valuing assets, that a number of assets in companies have <u>a great deal of</u> option value. And so the option theory that you've been looking at can also be applied to <u>real assets</u> instead of just <u>financial assets</u>. And that, in raising money, companies particularly have <u>a lot more to offer</u> from an option pricing perspective than they first thought. The idea on real options is that management is not just a passive participant, but that management can take <u>an active role</u> in making and revising decisions that can lead on from unexpected market developments such as, for example, the <u>price of oil</u> has gone up from $85 a barrel to <u>in excess of</u> $100 a barrel over the last year. So, if you were an oil producer this time last year, you would be taking a very different view on the <u>market for oil</u>. So the increase in oil prices has uncovered <u>a stream of options</u> which make oil producers a lot more valuable, and now you can bring oilfields <u>back on stream</u> that were not necessarily economic. So this is the kind of idea that when we're looking at a project, we're not just looking <u>at a static cash flow</u>, we're actually looking at a cash flow that can be subject to a lot of optionality.

Extension activity

Students could read the text to each other trying to link as many words together as possible.

Unit summary

These activities will give the students a chance to reflect on their attitude to note-taking and their ability to take effective notes. Having done the activities, they will probably have issues they wish to discuss further.

1. **Answers:**
    a. 1. saves time.
    b. 3. you must understand them.

2. Students can discuss their answers in pairs and make a plan of action for improving their performance in this area.

3. **Possible answers:**
    a. M
    b. L
    c. M
    d. L
    e. M

<u>Integrated Transport Policy (ITP)</u>

UK roads overcrowded → effects

- economic; ↘ prod.vity
- environmental; poll., glob. warming
- health probs.; lung, heart disease

Not one solution,

- e.g., road–building not solution, bec. → more traffic
- but range of measures needed (ITP)
- transport = political issue

1997 Public consult. on ITP

- One issue: encourage drivers to use publ. transp?
- Not enough, bec. drs. will still prefer to use cars.

Not one solution, but <u>package</u>, e.g.;

- car–sharing; lanes for use by cars with more than 1 person
- congestion charging; charging cars to enter some zones. Reduces no. of cars + income can be invested in publ. transp.

Schemes put pressure on drs.

- coalition wants to dev rail network – connect N/S Engl. + new airport

PHOTOCOPIABLE

Appendix 5b

Symbol	Meaning	Symbol	Meaning
↗	increase, rise, go up	≠	does not equal/is the opposite of
↘	fall, drop, decline, go down	€	euro
→	lead to, result in ...	?	I don't understand this.
←	caused by, result from..	!	This is surprising.
≥	is more than or equal to		

PHOTOCOPIABLE

Extract 1

3 purposes of education (Littlewood, 1992):

1. to pass on value, knowl. + cult.

2. to prepare Ss as members of soc.

3. humanistic; to develop indiv. to fulfil their potential

Extract 2

early 70s econ. boom → infl. in world econ.

1971 US $ left gold standard > $ effectively devalued

(1970 US econ = 1/3 world econ.)

Exch. rates floated → major industr. economies' infl. rates ↗ to 10, 15, 20%

1971 UK infl. rate = 25%!!!

Appendix 5d

Linear

<u>Health in dev.ed world, esp. UK</u>

- Life expectancy ↗ , taking more drugs, controlling many illnesses BUT not avoiding getting sick
- UK life expectancy; deaths of men 35–74 ↘ 42% 1990–2000
  Reason: taking more drugs
  e.g., prescr. of drugs for heart disease ↗ X 4 in last 20 years
- Need to tackle <u>causes</u> of heart disease
  1 physical inactivity (people walking ↘, cycling ↘ but driving ↗)
  2 unhealthy diet → obesity, % of obese adults → X 2 in last 12 yrs
- cf Norway – deaths of men 35–74 ↘ 54% 1990–2000

Mind map

<u>Health in dev.ed world, esp. UK</u>

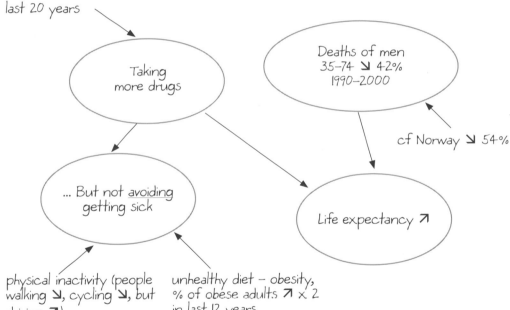

PHOTOCOPIABLE

	Advantages	Disadvantages
Linear notes	<ul><li>More familiar format</li><li>Easier to carry over to next page</li><li>Better for lectures arranged chronologically</li><li>Better for a lecture which contrasts different methods/theories – can do linear notes but side by side</li></ul>	<ul><li>If you miss something out, it can be difficult to find a space in which to insert it</li></ul>
Mind maps	<ul><li>Visually appealing</li><li>Better for showing sense relationships</li><li>May be more suitable for lectures which lack clear organization</li><li>Easier to revise from</li><li>Easier to remember, especially for people with good visual memories</li></ul>	<ul><li>How do you link ideas if you have to carry over to a new page?</li><li>Ideas not always organized clearly</li></ul>

PHOTOCOPIABLE

Appendix 5f

Answers:

I'm going to go through the theory of real options, and then I'm going to show you how they can be used to <u>raise some money</u>, particularly on property assets. 'Real options' is a term which was coined ten or 15 years ago, when people began to realize that <u>net present value</u> isn't the only thing you should look at in valuing assets, that a number of assets in companies have <u>a great deal of</u> option value. And so the option theory that you've been looking at can also be applied to <u>real assets</u> instead of just <u>financial assets</u>. And that, in raising money, companies particularly have <u>a lot more to offer</u> from an option pricing perspective than they first thought. The idea on real options is that management is not just a passive participant, that management can take <u>an active role</u> in making and revising decisions that can lead on from unexpected market developments such as, for example, the <u>price of oil</u> has gone up from $85 a barrel to <u>in excess of</u> $100 a barrel over the last year. So, if you were an oil producer this time last year, you would be taking a very different view on the <u>market for oil</u>. So the increase in oil prices has uncovered <u>a stream of options</u> which make oil producers a lot more valuable, and now you can bring oilfields <u>back on stream</u> that were not necessarily economic. So this is the kind of idea that when we're looking at a project, we're not just looking <u>at a static cash flow</u>, we're actually looking at a cash flow that can be subject to a lot of optionality.

PHOTOCOPIABLE

6 Introducing new terminology

In this unit students will:

- listen to different lectures introducing new terms or concepts
- meet different techniques for introducing new concepts
- practise recognizing unstressed function words which may be difficult to hear

Task 1 Introducing new terminology

The aim of this task is to introduce students to the ways in which lecturers use terminology.

1.1 Refer to recent lectures in the lecture cycle. Ask the students to think of any technical terms the lecturers have introduced and ask how the lecturers explained these. Then refer students to the list in the Course Book and ask them if the lecturers used any of these techniques, or other techniques. The list is not intended as an exhaustive one, and you and the students may like to add to it as you listen to different lectures in the course. If students struggle to remember technical terms or techniques, you could select words and techniques and make a matching activity.

Task 2 Embedded words

The aim of this task is to give students experience of listening to a lecture which includes technical terminology.

2.1 ▶ **CD2: 1 Answer:** The students should have made note of the fact that *responsibility* appears to contain words like *response* and *ability*, as well as words that are not related to the meaning, such as *sponsor* and *bill*.

2.2 Embedded words here refers to the smaller words apparently contained within polysyllabic words, e.g., *bed* within *embedded* or *response* within *responsibility*. Embedded words can be confusing to students as they may hear *response* rather than *responsibility* and try to construct a meaning with that word.

2.3 You may like to give students a few minutes to come up with other examples of multisyllable words with embedded words, e.g., a***band***on, **draw***backs*, ap***praise***, etc. If students are unable to think of any, you could give them a list of embedded and non-embedded words to select from.

Task 3 Introducing terms and concepts (1)

The aim of this task is to show students how lecturers introduce terms and concepts.

Pre-listening task
You may try to elicit what students know about the structure of the EU or simply have them read the introduction to this task with the definitions of the various institutions. Depending on the

students' background knowledge, you may need to give an overview of the EU to facilitate their understanding of the lecture.

3.1   Students can check the vocabulary in pairs or in their dictionaries.

3.2   ▶ **CD2: 2 Answers:**

	Matters they deal with	Who issues them	When they become legally binding
Regulations	minor technical matters, e.g., the amount of real cream in ice cream	the Commission or the Council of Ministers	when they are published in the *Official Journal*
Directives	for important measures*	the Council of Ministers	only binding when put into national law by individual parliaments of the member countries

* Has to be inferred from the text.

3.3   You may choose to do this exercise with students simply comparing notes, or, if you think your students are capable of it, ask them to take turns to explain fully the two terms by using their notes.

Alternatively, you may like to have a transfer activity, asking students to describe how laws are enacted in their own countries.

Task 4	Introducing terms and concepts (2)

The aim of this task is to show students the techniques lecturers use to define terminology.

Note: The term *monopoly* refers to a market in which one company has complete control because it is the only supplier of a product. A *dominant* company is one which has a very large share of a market; other companies operate in the market, but have a much smaller market share. The lecturer suggests that real monopolies are very rare, but dominance of companies is very common.

4.1   Some of your students may already be familiar with the term *monopoly*, especially if they are going on to study economics or investment banking. Some may also be able to explain *dominance*, or at least speculate on what it might mean. Encourage such students to explain the terms to the other students before listening to the extract.

4.2   The only phrase here that might cause problems is *not vulnerable to competition*, which suggests that a company has such control of a market that no other company can challenge it. You may want to prepare some examples from outside the field of the lecture to help students with comprehension.

4.3 ▶ **CD2: 3 Note:** *high entry barriers* might refer to such things as the high initial capital investment necessary for a company to enter the market.

Possible answers (see Appendix 6a, page 64):

Monopoly: market in which one company has sole control; very high entry barriers so company is not vulnerable to competition. Very rare in real world.

Dominance: where one company has very large share of market; other companies operate in the market, but have much smaller share, e.g., dominant company more than 50 per cent, perhaps a lot more, and second company, e.g., under 10 per cent. Very common in real world.

4.4 Students may come up with examples like Apple or Coca-Cola as examples of very dominant companies.

Depending on the subjects your students are studying, you might like to spend some time discussing:

- how these companies have established their dominance
- how they maintain that dominance
- in what kind of markets you find such dominance
- in what markets you do not find such dominance, e.g., air travel
- whether dominance is good for a) the consumer, b) society
- dominant companies and monopolies in their own countries

Task 5	Microskills: Weak forms of function words

This task focuses on recognizing the weak forms of function words such as articles, auxiliaries and prepositions.

**5.1/
5.2** ▶ **CD2: 4** Students should have no difficulty hearing the differences in pronunciation, but may not be able to explain why. You may have to do the first two as examples.

Answers:

1. **a.** /dəz/ is unstressed (weak form)
    b. /dʌz/ is stressed (strong form) to emphasize the positive verb form

2. **a.** /sʌm/ is stressed, to imply 'not all'
    b. /səm/ is unstressed

3. **a.** /fə/ is unstressed
    b. /fɔː/ is stressed; contrast with 'against'

4. **a.** /æt/ is stressed because it is the last word in the sentence.
    b. /ət/ is unstressed

5. **a.** /kən/ is unstressed
    b. /kæn/ is stressed to emphasize ability, in contrast to volition

6. **a.** /ʌs/ is stressed, to contrast with 'the students'
    b. /əs/ is unstressed

5.3   ▶ **CD2: 5** This consolidates work done in the microskills section of the previous unit. Students will have to identify word boundaries and recognize weak forms of function words. Although students may find it difficult to hear some words, they should be able to work them out from the context.

This is another extract from the same market research lecture used in Unit 4.

You may want to give students practice in weak forms by having them read the text aloud to each other after the exercise.

Answers (see Appendix 6b, page 65):
Multiple-choice questions – dead easy. They reduce interviewer bias; very easy for people to … very easy and fast for people to answer; very <u>easy for data processing</u>. But the argument goes that they are rather difficult to design. The thing about multiple-choice questions is that <u>you are forcing</u> people into certain answers. This is a good <u>reason for piloting</u>. If you have a multiple-choice question and you pilot it, you may find that people are not, they don't put the issue that you're asking them into that particular <u>set of categories</u> that you've imposed. So that's where <u>your pilots and qualitative research</u> will help. Let me just show you an example of this.

Unit summary

Answers:
1. a. 3
    b. 4
    c. 1
    d. 2

Extension activity
Have students choose a technical term and devise the same activity for another student. This could be turned into a class quiz or team game.

2. Answers depend on students.

3. a. The function words that would normally be unstressed in this sentence are: *a, of, that, can, for, to.* Categories of function words are: prepositions, pronouns, auxiliary verbs, conjunctions, grammatical articles or particles.
    b. Answers depend on students.
    c. Because they can carry some of the meaning.

Possible answers:

Monopoly: market in which one company has sole control; very high entry barriers so company is not vulnerable to competition. Very rare in real world.

Dominance: where one company has very large share of market; other companies operate in the market, but have much smaller share, e.g., dominant company more than 50 per cent, perhaps a lot more, and second company, e.g., under 10 per cent. Very common in real world.

PHOTOCOPIABLE

Appendix 6b

Answers:

Multiple-choice questions – dead easy. They reduce interviewer bias; very easy for people to … very easy and fast for people to answer; very <u>easy for data processing</u>. But the argument goes that they are rather difficult to design. The thing about multiple-choice questions is that <u>you are forcing</u> people into certain answers. This is a good <u>reason for piloting</u>. If you have a multiple-choice question and you pilot it, you may find that people are not, they don't put the issue that you're asking them into that particular <u>set of categories</u> that you've imposed. So that's where <u>your pilots and qualitative research</u> will help. Let me just show you an example of this.

PHOTOCOPIABLE

7 What lecturers do in lectures

In this unit students will:

- think about how lecturers organize information in their lectures
- discuss other ways of organizing information
- practise note-taking
- learn how word stress and pronunciation vary within word families

Introduction

Discourse structures may be less evident in lectures than in written texts but, in most cases, lectures do have some underlying structure. Recognizing this structure may help students understand the main ideas that the lecturer is trying to communicate. It will help students to monitor their own understanding of lectures if they are constantly asking the following questions:

- What is the lecturer doing at this point in the lecture?
- How does this part of the lecture relate to the other parts of the lecture?

If the students ask themselves these questions they may get the 'big picture' – i.e., the main ideas – of the lecturer's argument, rather than just a lot of detail.

Task 1 Macrostructure of lectures

This task focuses on raising students' awareness of the different types of organization of lectures.

Before referring to the Course Book, elicit from the students the kind of discourse structures they have come across in their writing classes, e.g., *SPSIE = situation–problems–solutions–implications of solutions–evaluation of solution*. Point out that in lectures, as in many written texts, different parts of the lecture may have different structures. For example, the first part of a lecture might be SPSIE, but the next part might be contrasting different theories, or tracing the history of a subject or outlining the advantages or disadvantages of different methods, etc.

1.1   Go through the example structures in Task 1 with the whole group, making sure they understand the language. Then ask them to do Ex 1.1 in pairs or small groups and report back to the whole class. If students are unable to answer the questions, refer them to the lectures in previous units and ask them to identify the structures.

Task 2 Lecture structure (1): Doing market research

The aim of this task is to give students the experience of listening to a lecture delivered using structure 1.

This extract was taken from a lecture entitled *Questionnaire design and attitude management.* The lecturer looks at different ways of collecting data for market research, i.e., getting people's opinions about products, or information about their habits, e.g., their shopping habits.

In this extract, the lecturer talks about four different methods of collecting data and the advantages or disadvantages of those methods.

2.1 You might like to give students individual thinking time to look at the questions and check dictionaries before doing this exercise in groups or pairs. They can then report back in a plenary session. In plenary discussion they may well come up with all the methods mentioned in this extract.

Note: You may wish to ensure that students understand the meaning of *bias*, and recognize that it is both a verb and a noun.

2.2 ▶ **CD2: 6 Notes:**

1. The lecturer refers to a visual or slide where the methods are listed. Hence she begins by saying *These are the four most common ways …*

2. She says she will talk about four methods, but says very little about pure telephone interviewing and concentrates more on computer-assisted telephone interviewing. You might like to point out to students before they listen that they will hear very little information about one of the methods.

Answers:
- computer-assisted telephone interviewing (CATI)
- postal questionnaires
- personal interviewing
- telephone interviewing

2.3 Check students understand the meaning of *implications*; use an example if students are unclear.

▶ **CD2: 6 Answers (see Appendix 7a, page 73):**
Students should come up with some or all of these points.

CATI:
- increasing in importance and coverage
- data entry at same time as asking questions
- some analysis can happen immediately
- huge savings in time
- computer can skip sections of questionnaire, depending on answers

Postal questionnaires:
- need to be very accurate
- no help available for respondent
- there may be follow-ups, but accuracy very important

Personal interviews:
- very high response levels – higher than other methods
- problem of bias
- very expensive

Telephone interviewing:
- less expensive, but lower response rate
- problem of bias
- can avoid bias by using strict schedule, but affects quality of data

The aim of this task is to give students the experience of listening to a lecture delivered using structure 2.

This extract was taken from a lecture given in the Psychology Department at the University of Reading, entitled *Observational or social learning*. In the lecture, the speaker reviews both anecdotal evidence and experimental evidence which test the hypothesis that animals learn from observing each other.

In this extract she is talking about experiments with monkeys, carried out by a researcher called Mineka.

The experiment took a group of 'naïve' monkeys who had, for example, been brought up in zoos. The monkeys had never encountered snakes before and therefore had no fear of them. The naïve monkeys observed a group of monkeys brought up in the wild in India who were afraid of snakes. The naïve monkeys were tested both before and after the observation is carried out, in order to see if they had learnt anything.

In this extract, the lecturer explains how the monkeys were tested and what the results suggest. Two experiments were used to test whether and what they learnt. The first experiment was a 'choice circus' – the speaker does not explain why it is called a 'choice circus', but this is a round arena, which presumably the monkeys cannot leave until the experiment is over. The second experiment involves an apparatus called a 'Wisconsin test apparatus', which she describes.

3.1 Again you may like to give students individual thinking time to look at these questions before discussing the questions in groups.

3.2 ▶ **CD2: 7** Allow the students to look through the exercise and ask questions about any of the language. Encourage them to speculate on why the animals would need to be pre-tested and have a follow-up test. Students should also think about signposting language and try to predict how the speaker will connect the stages of the experiment.

Students listen, make notes and then compare notes in pairs. If appropriate, play the extract again.

Answers (see Appendix 7b, page 74):
Students' notes should contain the following information.

Experimental situation:

Observer monkeys who were not afraid of snakes were allowed to watch wild monkeys who were afraid of snakes.

Timetable of experiment:

1. **Pre-test:** before the observer monkeys watched the wild monkeys, to check that they didn't have an in-built fear of snakes.
   Note: the reason for the pre-test is not mentioned in the text, but may come up in the discussion.

2. **Post-test:** immediately after, the monkeys watched the demonstrator monkey acting afraid of snakes.

3. **Follow-up test:** three months later to see if the learning had persisted, i.e., were they still afraid of snakes?

3.3   Note that a *neutral stimulus* here means an object which will neither especially attract nor frighten the monkeys.

Students listen, make notes and label the diagram, and then compare notes in pairs. If appropriate, play the extract again.

Answers (see Appendix 7b, page 74):

Procedure of experiments:

Choice circus

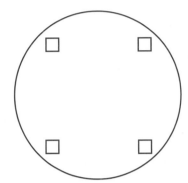

Wisconsin test apparatus

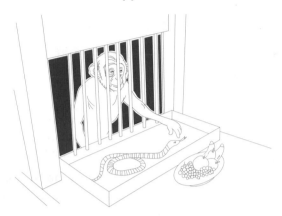

3.4   ▶ **CD2: 8** Students listen, make notes and then compare notes in pairs. If appropriate, play the extract again.

Answers (see Appendix 7c, page 75):

Students' notes should contain the following information.

Results:

The demonstrators (the monkeys brought up in the wild): spend almost no time near the real or toy snake.

The observers (the monkeys brought up in zoos): in the pre-test spend their time equally between the four stimuli; they show no avoidance of snakes at all. In the post-test they behave more like the model monkeys (not as frightened, but almost); they spend very little time near the snake. Their fear is just as strong three months later.

Conclusion:

Monkeys can learn by watching other monkeys. They don't have to be attacked or bitten by snakes – watching frightened monkeys is enough.

Task 4	Lecture structure (3): Contestable markets

The aim of this task is to give students the experience of listening to a lecture delivered using structure 3.

The original lecture was given in the Economics Department at the University of Reading, with the lecturer talking about different types of markets. It is from the same lecture that was used in Unit 6 when the lecturer discussed monopolies and dominance.

Note: The theory of contestable markets suggests that they are self-regulating, because other companies can easily move into the market. The result should be that the companies already in the market have to remain competitive and keep prices down because they might lose part of their market share to a new supplier.

4.1 Students can do this in pairs – the terms should be familiar to students of economics, banking or marketing, but may be unfamiliar to students from other disciplines. For these cases, the following definitions may be helpful:

Sunk costs are costs that are incurred before any profits can be made – for example, spending on advertising or researching a product idea. Once this money is spent, it cannot be retrieved. These costs can be a barrier to entry to a new market. Potential entrants faced with such costs, which cannot be recovered if entry failed, may be scared off.

Oligopolies occur when a few companies dominate a market. Often they work together as if they were a single monopoly. Alternatively, they may cooperate informally, agreeing not to compete on price rather than waging a price war.

Remember that the students are listening to answer the question. They should take notes to help them remember the content. Pairs should discuss their answers to the question as well as comparing their notes.

4.2 ▶ **CD2: 9** Students listen and make notes, then compare notes in pairs. It will probably be necessary to play the extract a second time. If students struggle with the content of listening, put some more information on the board to guide their listening.

Answers (see Appendix 7d, page 76):
Students' notes should contain the following information.

What the theory predicts:
- If incumbent companies raise their prices, new companies can enter the market and undercut them.
- If the incumbent company or companies cut their prices, the new company can leave the market with a profit.
- Knowing that new companies can easily come in encourages incumbent companies to keep prices down.
- Result: not necessary to have policies to control this kind of market.

Problems with the theory:
- If you change the assumptions slightly, the predictions change dramatically. The theory is not stable.
  Example:
  If there are delays for a new company coming into the market and it incurs sunk costs, the incumbent company can keep its prices high until the new company actually enters the market – then drop price to marginal costs.
  - entrant makes no money, in fact, loses money
  - new companies don't enter the market!

Task 5	Microskills: Word families (2)

This task consolidates and extends the work done in Unit 3 on word families.

5.1 You could also work on pronunciation of these noun forms, checking that students understand that the word stress generally falls on the syllable before these suffixes.

Answers:

~tion/~sion	~ance/~ence	~ment	~al	~ure
conclusion integration deduction consumption acquisition competition conversion combination	existence resistance	requirement amendment achievement	removal dismissal approval	failure procedure

Draw students' attention to spelling changes and test them on the words as part of the unit summary.

5.2   ▶ **CD2: 10** This exercise focuses on the use of verb and noun forms from the same word family as an aspect of lexical cohesion in a listening text. It starts with brief note-taking tasks before focusing on the language. If you think your students may find the note-taking too difficult, you could give them gapped texts.

Answers (see Appendix 7e, page 77):
Students' notes should look something like this.

Topic	Your notes	Verb and noun from same family
1. earthquakes in the UK	earthquakes (relatively) rare in UK, low magnitude, so often not recognized as earthquakes	occur/ occurrence
2. hospital workers and radiation	hospital workers exposed to low levels of radiation. Important to keep expos. to minimum	exposed/exposure
3. Japan's electronics industry	postwar Japan > developed electronics industry > industry strong competition for European manufacturers	emerged/ emergence
4. poverty	assumption that poverty exists only in dev.ing countries > needs of urban poor in dev.ed countries neglected	assumed/ assumption
5. behaviour of particles	particles collide at nr speed of light > massive amounts of energy released	collide/ collision
6. road safety schemes	tried to involve parents in road safety scheme, bec. involvement of local community is essential	involve/ involvement

7.	male lions in Africa	male lions in diff. parts of Africa behave in diff. ways when faced with danger. Environmental factors account for diff?	behave/behaviour
8.	financial products	study of performance of fin. products over 3 years. Some performed much better than others	perform/ performance

5.3 ▶ **CD2: 11** This exercise focuses on the use of synonyms as an aspect of lexical cohesion in a text. Students could predict as many possible answers before listening. For lower-level groups you could mention that the synonyms are all different parts of speech.

Answers (see Appendix 7f, page 78):

1. Many people are <u>worried</u> that young people lack strong role models, and this <u>concern</u> has prompted the police to question the conduct of professional footballers, whose actions may have a significant influence on young men.

2. The USA decided to <u>stay away from</u> the Moscow Olympics in 1980, in protest at the Soviet Union's invasion of Afghanistan. Four years later, the Soviet Union retaliated with its own <u>boycott</u> of the Los Angeles Olympics.

3. Many multinational companies prefer to <u>team up with</u> local enterprises. Such <u>alliances</u> have a number of advantages.

4. The public's <u>perception</u> of the government's handling of the economy was critical. While the economy had in fact grown by 2%, people <u>viewed</u> the high unemployment rate and the government's inability to control strikes as indicators of poor performance.

Extension activity

For higher-level groups, you could ask students to reformulate the sentences – swapping the synonyms around. This would enable them to see how the sentence structure would change.

Unit summary

1. **Possible answers:**
   You will know where the lecturer is in her/his lecture.
   You will understand better how one part of the lecture relates to another (how each part relates to the preceding one and the one that follows).
   You will understand the 'big picture' better if the various parts are logically ordered.
   You will be better able to predict what is going to come next in the lecture.
   You will better understand which part of an issue a key point relates to.

2. **Answers:**
   Lecture 1: 1c, 2d, 3a, 4b
   Lecture 2: 1c, 2a, 3b

3. **Answers:**
   Answers depend on students.

Appendix 7a

Answers:

CATI:

- increasing in importance and coverage
- data entry at same time as asking questions
- some analysis can happen immediately
- huge savings in time
- computer can skip sections of questionnaire, depending on answers

Postal questionnaires:

- need to be very accurate
- no help available for respondent
- there may be follow-ups, but accuracy very important

Personal interviews:

- very high response levels – higher than other methods
- problem of bias
- very expensive

Telephone interviewing:

- less expensive, but lower response rate
- problem of bias
- can avoid bias by using strict schedule, but affects quality of data

PHOTOCOPIABLE

Experimental situation:

Observer monkeys who were not afraid of snakes were allowed to watch wild monkeys who were afraid of snakes.

Timetable of experiment:

1. **Pre-test:** before the observer monkeys watched the wild monkeys, to check that they didn't have an in-built fear of snakes.
   Note: the reason for the pre-test is not mentioned in the text, but may come up in the discussion.

2. **Post-test:** immediately after, the monkeys watched the demonstrator monkey acting afraid of snakes.

3. **Follow-up test:** three months later to see if the learning had persisted, i.e., were they still afraid of snakes?

Procedure of experiments:

Choice circus

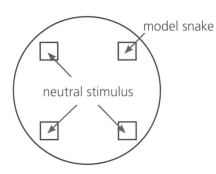

model snake

neutral stimulus

Wisconsin test apparatus

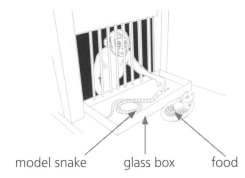

model snake   glass box   food

Appendix 7c

Answers:

Results:

The demonstrators (the monkeys brought up in the wild): spend almost no time near the real or toy snake.

The observers (the monkeys brought up in zoos): in the pre-test spend their time equally between the four stimuli; they show no avoidance of snakes at all. In the post-test they behave more like the model monkeys (not as frightened, but almost); they spend very little time near the snake. Their fear is just as strong three months later.

Conclusion:

Monkeys can learn by watching other monkeys. They don't have to be attacked or bitten by snakes – watching frightened monkeys is enough.

Answers:

What the theory predicts:

- If incumbent companies raise their prices, new companies can enter the market and undercut them.
- If the incumbent company or companies cut their prices, the new company can leave the market with a profit.
- Knowing that new companies can easily come in encourages incumbent companies to keep prices down.
- Result: not necessary to have policies to control this kind of market.

Problems with the theory:

- If you change the assumptions slightly, the predictions change dramatically. The theory is not stable.
  Example:
  If there are delays for a new company coming into the market and it incurs sunk costs, the incumbent company can keep its prices high until the new company actually enters the market – then drop price to marginal costs.
  - entrant makes no money, in fact, loses money
  - new companies don't enter the market!

PHOTOCOPIABLE

Appendix 7e

Topic	Your notes	Verb and noun from same family
1. earthquakes in the UK	earthquakes (relatively) rare in UK, low magnitude, so often not recognized as earthquakes	occur/ occurrence
2. hospital workers and radiation	hospital workers exposed to low levels of radiation. Important to keep expos. to minimum	exposed/ exposure
3. Japan's electronics industry	postwar Japan > developed electronics industry > industry strong competition for European manufacturers	emerged/ emergence
4. poverty	assumption that poverty exists only in dev.ing countries > needs of urban poor in dev.ed countries neglected	assumed/ assumption
5. behaviour of particles	particles collide at nr speed of light > massive amounts of energy released	collide/ collision
6. road safety schemes	tried to involve parents in road safety scheme, bec. involvement of local community is essential	involve/ involvement
7. male lions in Africa	male lions in diff. parts of Africa behave in diff. ways when faced with danger. Environmental factors account for diff?	behave/ behaviour
8. financial products	study of performance of fin. products over 3 years. Some performed much better than others	perform/ performance

PHOTOCOPIABLE

Answers:

a. Many people are <u>worried</u> that young people lack strong role models, and this <u>concern</u> has prompted the police to question the conduct of professional footballers, whose actions may have a significant influence on young men.

b. The USA decided to <u>stay away from</u> the Moscow Olympics in 1980, in protest at the Soviet Union's invasion of Afghanistan. Four years later, the Soviet Union retaliated with its own <u>boycott</u> of the Los Angeles Olympics.

c. Many multinational companies prefer to <u>team up with</u> local enterprises. Such <u>alliances</u> have a number of advantages.

d. The public's <u>perception</u> of the government's handling of the economy was critical. While the economy had in fact grown by 2%, people <u>viewed</u> the high unemployment rate and the government's inability to control strikes as indicators of poor performance.

PHOTOCOPIABLE

8 Digressions

In this unit students will:

- look at examples of digressions in lectures
- examine how lecturers sometimes mark the digressions
- practise following the lecturer's main points
- practise note-taking
- learn a number of expressions commonly used in lectures

Task 1   Reasons for digressions

This task introduces students to reasons why lecturers make digressions in lectures.

Introduce the term *digression* and then try to elicit from students why lecturers might digress and what problems such digressions may cause them. Then have them check the list of reasons and problems in the Course Book.

1.1   Have the students discuss their own experiences in pairs or groups. Students may (or may not) be able to remember examples from recent lectures in the lecture cycle. If not, refer them to specific previous lectures using the transcript.

Task 2   Identifying digressions

The aim of this task is to show students how lecturers use language, intonation and pauses to highlight digressions.

2.1   Students read the text and answer the questions, then check in pairs.

Answers:
1. The lecturer digresses in order to tell the students there will be a handout, so they don't need to take notes.

2. a. 1
    b. 2
    c. 3
    d. With rising intonation and slightly louder.

2.2   ▶ **CD2: 12** Students may come up with different answers here. The simple answer is that there is one digression, beginning *but I would point out before I go on* … and ending with … *good place to go*. The function of the digression is to give a reference. It is also possible to see a second digression in: *and I'm going to talk about some fairly classic experiments in this lecture* …

2. The lecturer lexically marks the beginning of her digression with *before I go on* … and signals that she is returning to the main idea with *Anyway* … Students may also be able to identify from her intonation and pausing that she has finished her digression.

Task 3 Practice: Questionnaire design (1)

The aim of this task is to give students practice in identifying digression.

This is an extract from a lecture students have heard before. They will have listened to the final two paragraphs of the second extract before, but this should not make a difference to their ability to do the tasks here, which have a very different focus.

3.1 ▶ **CD2: 13** Do not advise students on the content of their notes, as Ex 3.2 asks them if they noticed the digression.

Sample notes (see Appendix 8a, page 86):

General design principles
- q's must be precise
- q's must be well-ordered
- you need to decide ordering very carefully
- presentation is important
- how to order questions to get optimum response

3.2 Students should use their notes to discuss questions 1–3. You may want to elicit answers from students at this point, but do not give the answers, as Ex 3.3 is the follow-up work to help students clarify Ex 3.2.

3.3 ▶ **CD2: 13 Answers:**
1. The lecturer digresses to give students information on how they will be assessed on the course. This would match the reason 'to give general information about the course' in Task 1 of the Course Book.
2. Students will be given a case study to evaluate, appraise and comment on. They will also be given data they can analyze to support their comments.
3. Students will not have to do a questionnaire.
4. They might have spoken to students who did the course in the previous year who did have to do a questionnaire.
5. It was extremely difficult to mark as students produced huge amounts of material.
6. Answers depend on students.

3.4 The speaker introduces the digression by saying *incidentally* and indicates the end of the digression by pausing and saying *so*.

Task 4 Practice: Questionnaire design (2)

The aim of this task is to give students further practice recognizing and understanding the reasons for digressions within lectures.

4.1 This task is intended to help students predict the content of the listening. Students may have already carried out their own surveys and so this may be a useful review for them. If not, ask them if they have ever been interviewed as part of a survey, and imagine what 'dos' and 'don'ts' the interviewers have been given.

Elicit suggestions from the students.

4.2 ▶ **CD2: 14** Depending on the level of your students, you may want to split the lecture up into sections.

Answers:
1. Very clear objectives as to what the questionnaire is designed to achieve.
2. b. the sort of questions they will have
    d. the flow of the questionnaire
3. If they go outside the university to do research.
4. They were told to only research people on the course.
5. Sex.
6. The students interviewed people in the town centre (downtown).
7. He hadn't cleared the research with the Ethics Committee because he didn't think the students were going outside the campus.
8. Because they are very close to the subject they are researching. They know what information they want, but they have to check the questionnaire actually works, that it gets the information they want.
9. a. problems with the <u>length</u> of the questionnaire
    b. <u>the style of particular</u> questions
    c. whether questions are <u>valid</u>

4.3 Questions 4, 5, 6 and 7 are all concerned with the digression.

Possible reasons for the digressions are: to amuse the students or to illustrate the importance of obtaining approval.

4.4 ▶ **CD2: 14** The speaker does not mark this digression lexically as in the first extract, but by pausing at the beginning of the digression. When he returns to his main points later he does so by using a sentence structure – *You need to pre-test the questionnaire* – similar to the one he used before the digression when making his earlier main points; this was *You need to say something about …*

| Task 5 | **Practice: Integrated rural development** |

5.1 **Note:** Before students do this exercise, elicit from them what they understand by *integrated rural development* and which parts of the world they think it is most relevant to.

As an alternative to discussing the listed points, you can ask students to list them according to the potential contribution to rural development, or select the three which they think would have most impact.

5.2 ▶ **CD2: 15** Although Ex 5.2 does not explicitly ask students to take notes, you should encourage them to do so in order to answer the questions in Ex 5.2.

Sample notes (see Appendix 8b, page 87):

Main idea of IRD = provide a package of assistance across the sectors when working with poor rural areas – gives synergy

Example:

Introduce new varieties of rice and fertilizer

At same time:

- Try to combat malaria, inoculate against disease, clean up water supply > better health, greater productivity
- Build access roads > improve prices, reduce isolation
- Adult literacy > read labels of agric products, etc.

Comments on IRD

- Very exciting
- Lots of resources – but only a few small areas
- Only 6 areas in all Kenya – not possible in whole country
- Successful – not sustainable

Conclusion

Good idea, good people involved, success at time, not sustainable

Answers:

All the activities from Ex 5.1 are referred to in the extract.

5.3 ▶ **CD2: 15** This exercise is intended to check that students have managed to understand all the main points, and how the details relate to the main points. In checking their notes in Ex 5.2, you may find that the students have understood all this and therefore there is no need to do Ex 5.3 in full. In this case, ask students to look at the questions and identify which ones probably relate to the digression (questions 8, 9, 10). They can then listen and check the answers to those questions alone.

Answers:

1. Work with the poor, and smallholders and deliver a package of assistance.

2. They would improve farmers' health and therefore allow them to work harder.

3. It improves access for the farmers (inferential answer: this would make it easier for them to take produce to market).

4. If farmers can read, they can understand written instructions on agricultural products.

5. There was synergy (more than its parts), lots of resources, exciting to work on it.

6. It would have been too expensive to extend it to all parts of the country.

7. It could only operate in a few areas.

8. Two or three filing cabinets full of documents relating to IRD.

9. Initially he left them; then he went through them; finally he threw them all away.

10. It reminded him that IRD had been a good idea, quite successful, but not sustainable (also that the documents represented part of the history of development).

5.4   This exercise is drawing students' attention to the structure of the extract. This should be reflected in their notes.

Answers:

1. Commenting on IRD programme: 5, 6, 7

2. Giving an extended example of how IRD might work in practice: 2, 3, 4

3. Explaining the rationale behind IRD: 1

4. Digressing: 8, 9, 10

5. Drawing a conclusion: 10

5.5   The digression illustrates that a good programme has not left any lasting impact – and that development needs to be sustainable. It is marked by a change of perspective. He has been talking as an outside observer, but now adopts a personal perspective with *when I arrived in*; *in my room*; *I left them*, etc.

If students find this exercise difficult, do it as a whole class by asking questions to lead them to the answer.

5.6   ▶ **CD2: 15** This task aims not only to teach students new phrases, but to remind them to look at listening texts as sources of useful new language.

You should encourage students to look back at listening texts from earlier in the Course Book to check for other useful phrases they should learn (if they have not already done so!)

Possible answers:

what on earth? – used to emphasize a question when the speaker is surprised or can see no obvious answer to the question

give you synergy – provide added energy or impact as a result of people or measures working together instead of individually

my goodness – a polite expression of surprise

it all went in the skip – everything was thrown into a container (of a type often used by builders) for large amounts of rubbish

a package of assistance – a number of measures intended to work together with the aim of improving the situation

on the grounds – for the reason

that complements the agricultural measures – that improves or adds to the effect of the agricultural measures

more than the sum of the parts – giving more as a group than the individual parts do (e.g., a team of ordinary players can be a excellent team)

with the benefit of hindsight – when one looks back on something that has happened it is easy to see the problems; at the time you are planning, these might not be obvious

a scale-neutral activity – an activity that will work equally well on small and larger scales

increase their yields – produce bigger harvests

1. what on earth?, my goodness, it all went in the skip

2. on the grounds, increase their yields, with the benefit of hindsight

3–4 Answers depend on students.

| Task 6 | Microskills: Common expressions in lectures |

This task focuses on raising students' awareness of expressions which are common in lectures.

Each task in this section starts with a note-completion exercise, before focusing on a number of expressions which commonly occur in the BASE corpus of lectures and which might cause students comprehension problems.

For each listening activity, students should complete the gapped text and discuss the meaning of the phrases in pairs or groups.

Depending on the background/world knowledge of your students, you may need to explain some of the concepts discussed in the lecture extracts before doing the activities.

6.1 ▶ **CD2: 16 Answers (see Appendix 8c, page 88):**

States can't <u>isolate</u> themselves from outside world.

Growth of <u>television/mass communication</u> → states can't <u>ignore</u> what is going on around them. <u>Public opinion</u> has become more important, and states must respond. Strict appl. of <u>power</u> is being eroded.

6.2 ▶ **CD2: 16 Answers (see Appendix 8c, page 88):**

I think that realism excludes the possibility – and it's a growing one – that states can simply isolate themselves from the outside world. The growth of television, the growth of mass communications, have meant that it's virtually impossible for states to ignore what's going on around them, and public opinion has become more important <u>in some respects</u> within states, forcing states to do things that they might not otherwise do. So the strict application of power <u>in terms of</u> maintaining the hierarchy, of ignoring the interests of others, is simply slowly being withered away.

- *in some respects* – in some ways, to a certain extent
- *in terms of* – in relation to, in connection with

6.3 ▶ **CD2: 17 Answers (see Appendix 8d, page 89):**

Scand. ideas impact on Br. office design. e.g., factors influencing unusual design of offices: <u>employment legislation; workers' council; employer + employee rights</u>

6.4 ▶ **CD2: 17 Answers (see Appendix 8d, page 89):**

… ten years later, therefore, we have the Scandinavian ideas impacting on British office design. Another illustration of that might be, you'll discover in <u>the course of</u> the lecture, that some of the factors which are driving the unusual, sometimes, configuration of office buildings on the Continent, not always but sometimes, are <u>to do with</u> employment legislation – workers' councils, employers' rights, employees' rights.

- *in the course of* – during
- *to do with* – related to, associated with

6.5 ▶ **CD2: 18 Answers (see Appendix 8e, page 90):**

1982–1992: <u>commercial banks</u> did not lend money to dev.ing world. Only lenders were:

- other governments

- <u>other aid agencies</u>

- multilateral agencies, e.g., <u>IMF, World Bank</u>

6.6 ▶ **CD2: 18 Answers (see Appendix 8e, page 90):**

Nineteen eighty-two. None of the commercial banks gave any money to the developing world for <u>the best part of</u> ten years after the '82 debt crisis. They got such a bad fright by the debt crisis they <u>more or less</u> ceased lending in the developing world. So the only people who were lending money to governments in the developing world from 1982 onwards were other governments, other aid agencies and other multilateral agencies like the IMF and the World Bank.

- *the best part of* – most of, the majority of (a period of time)
- *more or less* – almost

Unit summary

1. **Answers:**

Even when lecturers organize their lectures well, they will sometimes digress from the main point. This might be to <u>comment</u> further on the point they are making or in order to give a <u>reference</u> to a book on the topic. They might want to give you some information about the course you are studying or say something about the <u>management</u> of the lecture they are giving at that moment. Lecturers will often tell students a personal <u>anecdote</u> to illustrate a point they are making. When lecturers make digressions, it can create problems for listeners. To start with, you will need to <u>recognize</u> that there is a digression. Then you will need to decide whether the digression is important and whether you need to continue taking notes. Finally, you need to know when the lecturer has returned to the <u>main point</u>.

2. **Possible answers:**

Incidentally, Anyway

Sample notes:

<u>General design principles</u>

- q's must be precise
- q's must be well-ordered
- you need to decide ordering very carefully
- presentation is important
- how to order questions to get optimum response

PHOTOCOPIABLE

Appendix 8b

Sample notes:

Main idea of IRD = provide a package of assistance across the sectors when working with poor rural areas – gives synergy

Example:

Introduce new varieties of rice and fertilizer

At same time:

- Try to combat malaria, inoculate against disease, clean up water supply > better health, greater productivity
- Build access roads > improve prices, reduce isolation
- Adult literacy > read labels of agric products, etc.

Comments on IRD

- Very exciting
- Lots of resources – but only a few small areas
- Only 6 areas in all Kenya – not possible in whole country
- Successful – not sustainable

Conclusion

Good idea, good people involved, success at time, not sustainable

6.1 Answers:

States can't <u>isolate</u> themselves from outside world.

Growth of <u>television/mass communication</u> → states can't <u>ignore</u> what is going on around them. <u>Public opinion</u> has become more important, and states must respond. Strict appl. of <u>power</u> is being eroded.

6.2 Answers:

I think that realism excludes the possibility – and it's a growing one – that states can simply isolate themselves from the outside world. The growth of television, the growth of mass communications, have meant that it's virtually impossible for states to ignore what's going on around them, and public opinion has become more important <u>in some respects</u> within states, forcing states to do things that they might not otherwise do. So the strict application of power <u>in terms of</u> maintaining the hierarchy, of ignoring the interests of others, is simply slowly being withered away.

- *in some respects* – in some ways, to a certain extent
- *in terms of* – in relation to, in connection with

Appendix 8d

6.3 Answers:

Scand. ideas impact on Br. office design. e.g., factors influencing unusual design of offices: employment legislation; workers' council; employer + employee rights

6.4 Answers:

… ten years later, therefore, we have the Scandinavian ideas impacting on British office design. Another illustration of that might be, you'll discover in <u>the course of</u> the lecture, that some of the factors which are driving the unusual, sometimes, configuration of office buildings on the Continent, not always but sometimes, are <u>to do with</u> employment legislation; workers' councils, employers' rights, employees' rights.

- *in the course of* – during
- *to do with* – related to, associated with

PHOTOCOPIABLE

6.5 Answers:

1982–1992: <u>commercial banks</u> did not lend money to dev.ing world. Only lenders were:

- other governments
- <u>other aid agencies</u>
- multilateral agencies, e.g., <u>IMF, World Bank</u>

6.6 Answers:

Nineteen eighty-two. None of the commercial banks gave any money to the developing world for <u>the best part of</u> ten years after the '82 debt crisis. They got such a bad fright by the debt crisis they <u>more or less</u> ceased lending in the developing world. So the only people who were lending money to governments in the developing world from 1982 onwards were other governments, other aid agencies and other multilateral agencies like the IMF and the World Bank.

- *the best part of* – most of, the majority of (a period of time)
- *more or less* – almost

PHOTOCOPIABLE

These tracks are also available as video resources on the *EAS: Listening* DVD.

Unit 1: Listening and lectures

CD1 Track 1
Ex 2.2

Listen to Part 1 of a talk in which a lecturer describes some of the problems of listening. Then answer the following questions.

Part 1
Many students find listening to and understanding spoken English particularly difficult, and I think there are a number of reasons for this.

Firstly, there's the speed at which people talk. Obviously, when people are speaking quickly it's more difficult to understand them.

And then there's the issue of the topic that people are talking about. A topic you don't know much about is more difficult to understand than one you're familiar with. When you're listening to a familiar topic, you only need to concentrate on the new information, whereas if it's a new topic you often have to concentrate on just about everything.

There's also the problem of specialized vocabulary. There may be words you don't know. Now, if there's only a few words like this, people can generally follow the meaning, but if there are key words, or if there are a lot of unfamiliar words, then this can cause problems.

But there are two additional problems you may be faced with if English is not your first language.

When you're reading, you can see when one word ends and another one begins, because there's a space between them. But when you're listening, you can't. You often can't hear when one word ends and another begins, so you have to pick out the words you recognize and, from your understanding of the meaning, the context and your knowledge of English grammar, fill in the gaps.

When students learn English, they're generally reading texts rather than listening to them, so they get used to the written forms of words rather than the spoken forms. But when they learn these words, they build up in their mind an expectation of their pronunciation. And when they actually hear these words in natural speech, they often fail to recognize the words, because they're pronounced in an unexpected way.

So, there are two problems; firstly, it's difficult for students to know when one word ends and another begins, and secondly, they often fail to recognize words which they know in the written form.

CD1 Track 2
Ex 2.3

Now listen to Part 2 of the talk. The lecturer asks you to write down a phrase. Do this as you listen.

Part 2
So let's look at an example of this. I said earlier that students often fail to recognize words that they hear in natural speech. OK, so let's take the second part of that sentence, 'words they hear in natural speech'. Yeah? Now I'd like you to take a pen and a piece of paper and if you could write that bit of the sentence down for me please. Just 'words they hear in natural speech'. That part. OK? So you're writing down 'words they hear in natural speech'. OK, so how many words are there in that phrase? Are there three? Four? Five? In fact there are six. 'Words they hear in natural speech.' Now when I said this at normal speed, you may have heard 'hearinnatural' as one word, rather than three. And you may not have even recognized the word 'natural', because you had an expectation that it might be pronounced /ˈnætʃuræl/ or /ˈneɪtʃurəl/, instead of /ˈnætʃrəl/, which is how it is pronounced. You might have even heard the word *actual* or *national* instead of *natural*. But the point is, if you saw this phrase written down, you would probably understand the meaning, but when you hear it, it's more difficult for you to understand.

CD1 Track 3

Ex 2.4

Listen to Part 3 of the talk. Complete this excerpt by writing two to six words in each space.

Part 3

So what is the solution to these two problems? Well, firstly, you need to get as much practice listening to natural speech as possible. Listen to extracts from lectures and try to develop your understanding of how words and phrases are really pronounced, not how you expect them to be pronounced. And secondly, you need to accept that when you listen you may misunderstand what is being said. So you need to be ready to change your mind about your understanding of the meaning, if what you hear doesn't make sense compared to what you understood before. And this means taking a flexible, open-minded approach to listening.

CD1 Track 4

Ex 3.2

Listen to Part 1 of the talk and make notes about points 1–3.

Part 1

Good morning. I'm talking to you this morning because I'm interested in the differences between academic cultures in China and the UK. Now, what I mean by 'academic cultures' is simply how students study in the two countries – what are the different components of their courses, what teachers expect from them, and so on. And I'd like to present my ideas to you today and get some feedback from you. The thing I want to focus on particularly is lectures. I'm interested in the difference between lectures, both in terms of how the lectures are organized or presented and also in terms of how the lecture fits into the overall academic programme.

Now, the first question I need to address is, 'How do I know anything about lectures in China?' because I haven't studied there and in fact I haven't even been there. Well, I found out by interviewing Chinese students. What I did was conduct a so-called 'tracking study'. That means that you follow students over a period of time. What I did was to follow 12 Chinese students, all doing different courses, different master's courses at the University of Reading, and over their year of study I interviewed them three times individually. I interviewed them once

in the autumn term, once in the spring term and then again in the summer term. And the interviews lasted for about an hour, an hour and a quarter. I asked them a number of questions about studies in the UK and about their studies in China. So my information comes from them and so I have to say right from the beginning that I am talking here about information I got from 12 students, which is obviously a very small sample, and I don't know how representative what they said is of the Chinese education system as a whole. So we have to remember that limitation. I did choose different students from different parts of China, and I made sure that there was an equal number of men and women, and they were all studying different courses here at Reading, so there was a range of backgrounds and experience. But there is that limitation. However, I felt that what I was hearing from the students was actually very similar. I mean, what they were saying individually was more or less the same. So I felt that maybe there is some basis for what they said, and maybe what they did say and maybe their experience was not untypical, in general, of students in China.

CD1 Track 5

Ex 3.4

In Part 2 of the talk, the lecturer first talks about some of the characteristics of lectures in China and then compares these with lectures in the UK. Listen and make notes on the main points he makes.

Part 2

OK, so what did I find out? I think the first thing to say is that my impression is that in China the lecture delivers a lot of the content of the course, or the lecturer delivers a lot of the content of the course. And this seems to be especially true at undergraduate level. And just to reinforce this, the students I talked to were postgraduate students. In other words, they'd done undergraduate studies in China. I'm not sure about postgraduate studies in China. But what they said about undergraduate courses was that a lot of the course content came through the lectures. In other words, the students go to the lectures, they make notes in the lectures, and at the end of the term, or at the end of the year, if they have a test or examination, in many cases they simply give back to the lecturer what the lecturer gave to them during the lectures. And that seems to be sufficient to pass the exam and pass the course.

So, the lecture is the important vehicle of the course content; it carries the course content.

Now, the second point they made about lectures was that in China they don't seem to be very interactive, in the sense that students sit, they listen, they make lots and lots of notes. But they don't often ask questions during the lecture or at the end of the lecture, and they don't have much discussion, either during or at the end of the lecture, and that is not expected of them. So they really, in China, lectures don't seem to be very interactive.

Another point which students made to me, which I thought was interesting, was that the main points, the important points of a lecture, are often explicitly marked by the lecturer. The lecturer might say, 'OK, this point is very important, make a note of this' and might even write things on the blackboard, which the students would copy down verbatim. In other words, they would copy down exactly what he was writing. So this was interesting, it seems that the students don't have to decide for themselves what is important, what is less important. The lecturer tells them. Now obviously that's a very general and very rough caricature of what students told me about Chinese lectures. But how does that compare with the UK situation?

Well, in the UK, I think it's fair to say that the course content is not only delivered through the lectures. If you study on a UK course and if you only give back to the lecturer in examinations, or tests, or assignments or essays, if you only give back what he or she says during the lecture, then I don't think you are going to pass the exam, the course. I think what lecturers are doing in the UK is something different. I think either they are giving an overview of the main ideas connected with the subject, or they are giving some general background to the subject, and then it's the student's responsibility to go away, and to do lots of reading, and to really fill in the details, and to fully understand the theories, the ideas the lecturer is talking about.

And that really brings me to the point of reading. Because what I understood from my Chinese students was that in China, certainly at undergraduate level, they had one course book for each course, and just to emphasize that, they seemed to have one course book. And there was a very close correspondence between what the lecturer was saying and what was in the course book. In other words, if the students wanted to, they could go away at the end of the lecture and read the course book, and it would essentially say what the lecturer himself had said, so there was that kind of reinforcement. In the UK it's very different. There's not one course book for one course. You can't just go away and read one book, and find the entire content of the lectures there. You will have to read a lot of books and a lot of articles to fill in what the lecturer has given you. So in the UK, reading, and reading really widely, is an essential part of what students do after lectures. In China it seems that there is a lot less reading, and the reading is mainly concentrated on this one course book.

That's one thing about the UK. The other thing about the UK, the UK lecture, is that lecturers here do expect students to interact, to ask questions, to raise points of view, to make comments, to enter into discussion. Now obviously how much discussion there is, how much interaction there is, depends very much on how many students there are in the lecture. Here at Reading, in some cases, we may have 20 students in a lecture and on other courses you may have 200 students in a lecture, and obviously there's less discussion if there are more students. There's less time for questions. But interactiveness in general is very important in the UK.

Well, those are just some of my impressions of the differences between lectures in China and the UK, but I would really be very interested now in hearing your opinions – whether you think what I've talked about is true from your experience or not.

Unit 2: Introductions to lectures

CD1 Track 6
Ex 1.4

Listen to the introduction. Then answer the questions.

Migration
There has been a lot of talk recently in the newspapers and on television about immigration to the UK from countries joining the EU, countries like Poland, and more recently Romania and Bulgaria. This discussion is centred on questions like whether this is good for the British economy or not – in terms of productivity, or impact on national infrastructure, for example, on the health and education services, etc. However, that's not the type of migration that I want to look at today. What I want to look at is internal migration, i.e., the movement of people from country to city, and vice versa, and from one city to another.

CD1 Track 7
Ex 3.2

Listen to the introduction to the lecture *Britain and the European Monetary Union*. Which functions from the checklist in Task 2 does the lecturer use?

Britain and the European Monetary Union
OK, good morning. Well, first up, can you all hear me? Good. Well that's a good place to start. Well, today I'm going to be talking to you mainly about Britain and the so-called Eurozone, the European Monetary Union. As I am sure you know there are currently, although this may have changed by the time you listen to the recording of this lecture, 17 countries in the Eurozone; the last country to join being Estonia in 2011. You also know, as you are living in the UK and are using British currency (pounds and pence) on a daily basis, that Britain decided not to join the Eurozone, and given the problems the euro has had over the last few years, and is still having, many British people consider that to have been the right decision. Incidentally, the UK is not alone in this, as other EU countries also opted out, for example, Denmark. I'll come back to the reasons the UK did not originally join later in this lecture.

Now I have already talked in previous lectures about the early history of the European Union, or the European Economic Community, as it was originally known. I also talked about the reasons Britain was reluctant to join the EEC, and why some other members of the EEC, France in particular, were not convinced that Britain should join either. One of the main reasons for this was, I suggested, that Britain felt it had a special arrangement with the United States and with its former colonies in the Commonwealth and didn't want to endanger this relationship by joining. And after Britain's participation in the wars with Iraq, you might conclude that the British still believe they have a special relationship with the US – even if the US may not see this in the same way.

However, leaving all that aside, today I want to talk about three things. Firstly, I am going to talk about the process of how the euro was introduced, and then I'm going to talk about the economic and political tests that a new country has to pass in order to join the euro – despite the problems in the Eurozone there are still countries that would like to join. However, as the title of my lecture suggests, I am going to spend most of the time today talking about why Britain did not adopt the euro, and what that said, and still says, about Britain's attitude in general to membership of the European Union.

CD1 Track 8
Ex 3.4

Listen to the introduction to the lecture *Globalization*. Which functions from the checklist in Task 2 does the lecturer use?

Globalization
Globalization is a term that you hear everywhere these days, whether people are talking about food – McDonald's and other fast-food companies in particular – or about the economy, with more and more multinational companies all over the world, or about information, with the Internet and the spread of the English language making the same information available at the same time to people all over the world. Arguably, globalization also includes national cultures, with some authorities suggesting, as I myself do in my latest book, that national cultures as we knew them no longer exist. In any case, globalization is often said to be the single most profound and wide-ranging change in human history. Ever. Well, that is something that you can discuss later – you may have your own opinions on whether this is true or not. But it does go without saying that it is something which affects everybody's life; it affects people as diverse as farmers in the Third World, stockbrokers in London and New York, or global tycoons in multimillion-dollar empire industries. So, obviously, there is something in which a political scientist, or, for that matter, an historian, or a sociologist, or a geographer, or a whole range of other disciplines, might well be interested.

What I'm going to try to do today is give you some understanding of the history of globalization, what globalization means to people on a local level and what its implications could be for the whole world.

So I'm going to be talking on a global scale – which is appropriate for this topic – and I'm also going to be covering some fairly long periods of time.

CD1 Track 9

Ex 3.6

Listen to the introduction to the lecture *Magistrates' courts*. Which functions from the checklist in Task 2 does the lecturer use?

Magistrates' courts

Good morning, everybody. In spite of what John just said, I'm not going to spend a lot of time talking about the family work. That's a specialist area of the Magistrates' court. As John says, it deals with non-criminal matters involving the state and children. So, for example, in the case of family break-up, it would involve making parental contact orders where the parents can't agree on how much contact time each parent should have with the child – after divorce, for example. It also deals with parental responsibility. So that means fathers who are refusing to pay for the maintenance of their children. Then, finally, it deals with any kind of case involving the state and the child – notably, when the state wishes to take the child from the care of the parents and put it in the care of somebody else or in the care of the local authority, the government, and also when the child is to be adopted by another family. But that is another specialist area. What we are mainly concerned with today is the criminal court, and that is what I am going to spend most of my time talking about this morning.

So this is a court – the Magistrates' court deals only with offences, criminal offences. So we're not dealing, for example, with disputes between neighbours. For example, if you have an argument with your neighbour about the noise that is being made, or the height of his hedge which is preventing the light getting into your garden – all those kinds of things are dealt with in the civil court, but here we are dealing with the criminal court, so it's crimes against the state as defined by the legal code. So I just want to make that clear from the beginning.

So within that criminal justice system, first of all we are dealing with England and Wales here. There is a slightly different system that operates in Scotland – so we're talking about England and Wales only. Within that justice system there are two main courts. One is the crown court which deals with very serious offences. So those would be the ones that you've probably all seen on television where there's a judge and 12 members of a jury. Those are only for serious offences. We are dealing with the lesser offences and those are dealt with in the courts that I'm going to talk to you about today, and that is the Magistrates' court.

CD1 Track 10

Ex 4.1

Listen and complete the sentence from the introduction to *Britain and the European Monetary Union*.

However, as the title of my lecture suggests, I am going to spend most of the time today talking about why Britain did not adopt the euro, and what that said, and still says, about Britain's attitude in general to membership of the European Union.

CD1 Track 11

Ex 4.2

Listen and complete the following sentences from the introduction to *Magistrates' courts*. Write one word in each space.

So, for example, in the case of family break-up, it would involve making parental contact orders where the parents can't agree on how much contact time each parent should have with the child …

What we are mainly concerned with today is the criminal court, and that is what I am going to spend most of my time talking about this morning.

CD1 Track 12

Ex 4.4

Listen to a recording about security and computers. Complete the text with one word in each space.

Security is an important aspect of using a computer that many people do not pay much attention to. If you buy a laptop or personal computer, you will probably want to connect to the Internet. If so, it is important that you install security software which will protect it from attack by viruses or spyware. Now there is a wide range of products available on the market which are relatively cheap and which provide a variety of different features. For example, in addition to checking their computer for viruses, parents can use the software to control which websites their children can access. You should not assume, however, that you are 100% safe if you are using such security software. You should make sure that you have backup copies of your work, and you should be very careful about keeping important information, such as bank account details, on your computer.

CD1 Track 13
Ex 4.5

Listen to a recording about competition between large supermarket chains and small local shops. Complete the text with one word in each space.

Because of planning restrictions, the large UK supermarket chains are looking to expand their businesses and increase profits by opening smaller 'convenience stores'. Organizations representing small, independent shops protest that they now face unfair competition from the large chains. And they accuse the large chains of a number of practices that make it difficult for them to compete. Firstly, it is alleged that below-cost pricing is used by large supermarkets to force smaller, local shops out of business. Secondly, the large chains often buy up land which is not immediately used, and this prevents smaller local businesses from entering the market.

There is also some concern that the large chains are treating their suppliers unfairly. Farmers claim that they are being paid less for their products, and they are reluctant to complain for fear of losing key contracts.

However, supermarkets argue that the consumer is the best regulator of the market.

CD1 Track 14
Ex 4.7

Listen to a recording about the effect of global warming on numbers of polar bears. Complete the text with one word in each space.

Wildlife experts predict that numbers of polar bears will decline by at least 50% over the next 50 years because of global warming. Polar bears rely on sea ice to catch seals for food, and it has emerged that ice floes in the Arctic are disappearing at an alarming rate. Now scientists report that the animals are already beginning to suffer the effects of climate change in some parts of Canada, and if there is any further delay in tackling this problem, polar bears may be extinct by the end of the century.

CD1 Track 15
Ex 4.8

Listen to a recording about monitoring water levels in rivers. Complete the text with one word in each space.

Scientists are now able to monitor river levels using information from satellites by using a computer programme devised by researchers at De Montfort University in Leicester. Satellites have been able to measure the height of the sea by timing how long it takes to receive a beam bounced back off waves. But, until now, interference from objects on the banks of rivers has made it impossible to measure river levels.

However, the new programme, which is based on data collected over the last decade, is specially designed to filter out this interference. This new technology will be particularly useful in monitoring river-levels in remote areas. It will, for example, enable scientists to examine river level patterns over the entire Amazon River basin, contributing towards our understandings of climate change.

Unit 3: Identifying key ideas in lectures

CD1 Track 16
Ex 2.2

Listen to Part 1 of the lecture, which is in three sections. Identify the three sections and number them in the correct order.

Franchising
Part 1
Section 1
The form of business development I'm going to look at now is franchising. The term 'franchising' covers a wide range of business arrangements, but today I'm going to focus on 'business format franchising'.

If you own a small or medium-sized enterprise, you may reach a stage in its development at which, in order to develop further, you need large amounts of capital, or you need to reorganize your business, or to bring into the management team new skills. Well, let's say you own four or five hairdressing salons in your city which are very profitable. You want to expand the business, but recognize firstly that a lot more money will need to be invested, and secondly that you will not be able to exert the same amount of personal control over the day-to-day running of the business that you've been used to. This stage in the growth of the business may present the entrepreneur with risks that he or she is unwilling to run. However, one way of minimizing such risks, while at the same time continuing to develop and profit from a successful brand, is by franchising your business.

Section 2

So, what is franchising? Well, here is a definition from the British Franchising Association website. And it says, 'Business format franchising is the granting of a licence by one person (the franchisor) to another (the franchisee), which entitles the franchisee to trade under the trademark/trade name of the franchisor and to make use of an entire package, comprising all the elements necessary to establish a previously untrained person in the business, and to run it with continual assistance on a predetermined basis.' This package would include things like training, consultancy arrangements, possibly supplies, marketing on a national scale, etc., etc.

Section 3

So, for example, if you own a group of successful fast-food restaurants trading under the same name, you may decide to run your business as a franchise. You would allow other businesspeople to open their own branches of the fast-food chain, using your trademark, and in fact you would probably supply a lot of the signage and materials necessary to maintain a uniform brand. In return, the franchisee pays you, the franchisor, an initial fee, that is to say a fee paid at the beginning of the business arrangement, and also an ongoing management service fee. This management service fee is related to the volume of business the franchisee is doing, so it might be calculated as a percentage of the turnover, or as a mark-up on supplies provided by the franchisor. So there are two kinds of fee: the one-off initial fee to set up the franchise, and the ongoing management service fee.

CD1 Track 17
Ex 2.3

Listen to Part 1, Section 1 again and answer the questions.

Section 1

The form of business development I'm going to look at now is franchising. The term 'franchising' covers a wide range of business arrangements, but today I'm going to focus on 'business format franchising'.

If you own a small or medium-sized enterprise, you may reach a stage in its development at which, in order to develop further, you need large amounts of capital, or you need to reorganize your business, or to bring into the management team new skills. Well, let's say you own four or five hairdressing salons in your city which are very profitable. You want to expand the business, but recognize firstly that a lot more money will need to be invested, and secondly that you will not be able to exert the same amount of personal control over the day-to-day running of the business that you've been used to. This stage in the growth of the business may present the entrepreneur with risks that he or she is unwilling to run. However, one way of minimizing such risks, while at the same time continuing to develop and profit from a successful brand, is by franchising your business.

CD1 Track 18
Ex 2.4

Listen to Part 1, Section 2 again and answer the following questions.

Section 2

So, what is franchising? Well, here is a definition from the British Franchising Association website. And it says, 'Business format franchising is the granting of a licence by one person (the franchisor) to another (the franchisee), which entitles the franchisee to trade under the trademark/trade name of the franchisor and to make use of an entire package, comprising all the elements necessary to establish a previously untrained person in the business, and to run it with continual assistance on a predetermined basis.' This package would include things like training, consultancy arrangements, possibly supplies, marketing on a national scale, etc., etc.

CD1 Track 19
Ex 2.5

Listen to Part 1, Section 3 again and answer the following questions.

Section 3

So, for example, if you own a group of successful fast-food restaurants trading under the same name, you may decide to run your business as a franchise. You would allow other businesspeople to open their own branches of the fast-food chain, using your trademark, and in fact you would probably supply a lot of the signage and materials necessary to maintain a uniform brand. In return, the franchisee pays you, the franchisor, an initial fee, that is to say a fee paid at the beginning of the business arrangement, and also an ongoing management service fee. This management service fee is related to the volume of business the franchisee is doing, so it might be calculated as a percentage of the turnover, or as a mark-up on supplies provided by the franchisor. So there are two kinds of fee: the one-off initial fee to set up the franchise, and the ongoing management service fee.

CD1 Track 20
Ex 3.2

Listen to Part 2 of the lecture.

Part 2
Section 1

There are a number of issues you need to consider when deciding whether or not to franchise your business. Firstly, there needs to be a relatively stable, long-term market for the product or service you are franchising. This is partially because substantial investment in time and money is required to set up and develop a franchise operation, and partly because you need an established market with potential for long-term growth to attract franchisees. So, something like a chain of hairdressing salons might offer potential for a franchise, because there will always be a demand for women to have their hair cut and styled. On the other hand, a franchise to promote and sell a new kind of children's toy might be less successful, because toys tend to have a short market lifespan.

Section 2

In addition – and this is fairly obvious – you will need a fairly wide margin between cost and income. Remember that the gross margin needs to provide a return on the investment to both the franchisor and the franchisee. So you will need to keep costs low and prices as high as the market will bear. One advantage of a franchise operation is that supplies can be bought in bulk across the whole franchise, which will help to keep costs down. But you can see that franchising would be unsuitable in a market where the margin between cost and income is very narrow.

Section 3

The franchisor will need to provide support and training to the franchisee because, in addition to the brand, what you are selling is a way of doing business that has proved successful. You will need to produce an operating manual that

describes in detail all the different systems and procedures involved in the business, and the performance and quality standards, but you will also have to provide some kind of training for the franchisees and possibly his employees, certainly in setting up the operation and possibly on a regular, ongoing basis. The important point here is that for a franchise to be successful, it should be possible for the franchisee to develop the skills required to operate the business fairly quickly. So, although some initial training may be required, the franchisee should be able to operate the business efficiently and successfully within a few months of start-up. In some types of franchise, the skills required may be acquired quickly; in others, the franchisee may have already developed most of the necessary skills in previous employment. So, for example, someone operating a franchise in the restaurant industry is likely to have experience either as an employee in a restaurant, or in a similar field.

CD1 Track 21
Ex 3.4

Listen to Part 2, Section 1 again and answer the following questions.

Section 1

There are a number of issues you need to consider when deciding whether or not to franchise your business. Firstly, there needs to be a relatively stable, long-term market for the product or service you are franchising. This is partially because substantial investment in time and money is required to set up and develop a franchise operation, and partly because you need an established market with potential for long-term growth to attract franchisees. So, something like a chain of hairdressing salons might offer potential for a franchise, because there will always be a demand for women to have their hair cut and styled. On the other hand, a franchise to promote and sell a new kind of children's toy might be less successful, because toys tend to have a short market lifespan.

CD1 Track 22
Ex 3.5

Listen to Part 2, Section 2 again and answer the following questions.

Section 2

In addition – and this is fairly obvious – you will need a fairly wide margin between cost and income. Remember that the gross margin needs to provide a return on the investment to both the franchisor and the franchisee. So you will need to keep costs low and prices as high as the market will bear. One advantage of a franchise operation is that supplies can be bought in bulk across the whole franchise, which will help to keep costs down. But you can see that franchising would be unsuitable in a market where the margin between cost and income is very narrow.

CD1 Track 23
Ex 3.6

Listen to Part 2, Section 3 again and answer the following questions.

Section 3
The franchisor will need to provide support and training to the franchisee because, in addition to the brand, what you are selling is a way of doing business that has proved successful. You will need to produce an operating manual that describes in detail all the different systems and procedures involved in the business, and the performance and quality standards, but you will also have to provide some kind of training for the franchisees and possibly his employees, certainly in setting up the operation and possibly on a regular, ongoing basis. The important point here is that for a franchise to be successful, it should be possible for the franchisee to develop the skills required to operate the business fairly quickly. So, although some initial training may be required, the franchisee should be able to operate the business efficiently and successfully within a few months of start-up. In some types of franchise, the skills required may be acquired quickly; in others, the franchisee may have already developed most of the necessary skills in previous employment. So, for example, someone operating a franchise in the restaurant industry is likely to have experience either as an employee in a restaurant, or in a similar field.

CD1 Track 24
Ex 4.1

Listen to Part 3 of the lecture. Make notes on the key points in your notebook.

Part 3
Section 1
One further issue you may need to consider is whether the business is transferable to another geographical area. If you have developed your business serving one particular part of the country and you want to set up a franchise network covering a much larger area – the whole country, for example – another thing you will have to consider is whether there is a similar market for your product or service in different regions. It may be, for example, that competition in other parts of the country may be so strong that it is difficult for franchisees to survive, or that for localized socioeconomic or cultural reasons the business may not be as profitable.

Section 2
Finally, when you are setting up a franchise network, you will need to bear in mind that you will be losing direct control of the way your brand is perceived by the customer, so this brings me to my last point, which is to emphasize the importance of protecting your brand. I am sure you are all aware that it often takes a long time to establish a distinctive brand with a valuable reputation, but that this reputation can be damaged comparatively quickly if, for example, quality standards are not consistently applied. The detailed operating manual, that I referred to earlier, will play a role in maintaining the brand but, just as important, you need to take care selecting franchisees and monitoring their operations. In addition to checking that franchisees have the relevant skills and experience to run a successful business, you also need to ensure that they share the same business values as you, that they accept the importance of maintaining the brand and that they are clear about what they can or can't change about the way the business is run – so people who are very individualistic will probably not make good franchisees.

Section 3
The written agreement between the franchisor and franchisee should specify very clearly what performance and quality standards are expected, and much of the initial training will be ensuring that staff have the skills to achieve these standards. However, regular visits to franchise units are essential in ensuring that the standards are being applied consistently and uniformly, and ongoing training may be necessary to deal with issues that are uncovered in these visits. Protecting the brand is ultimately in the interests of both the franchisor and the franchisee because, for the franchisee, one of the main advantages in running a franchise is that they are buying into and helping to consolidate an established brand.

CD1 Track 25

Ex 4.2

Listen to Part 3, Section 1 again and complete the excerpt with one to three words in each space.

Section 1

One further issue you may need to consider is whether the business is transferable to another geographical area. If you have developed your business serving one particular part of the country and you want to set up a franchise network covering a much larger area – the whole country, for example – another thing you will have to consider is whether there is a similar market for your product or service in different regions. It may be, for example, that competition in other parts of the country may be so strong that it is difficult for franchisees to survive, or that for localized socioeconomic or cultural reasons the business may not be as profitable.

CD1 Track 26

Ex 4.3

Listen to Part 3, Section 2 again.

Section 2

Finally, when you are setting up a franchise network, you will need to bear in mind that you will be losing direct control of the way your brand is perceived by the customer, so this brings me to my last point, which is to emphasize the importance of protecting your brand. I am sure you are all aware that it often takes a long time to establish a distinctive brand with a valuable reputation, but that this reputation can be damaged comparatively quickly if, for example, quality standards are not consistently applied. The detailed operating manual that I referred to earlier will play a role in maintaining the brand but, just as important, you need to take care selecting franchisees and monitoring their operations. In addition to checking that franchisees have the relevant skills and experience to run a successful business, you also need to ensure that they share the same business values as you, that they accept the importance of maintaining the brand and that they are clear about what they can or can't change about the way the business is run – so people who are very individualistic will probably not make good franchisees.

CD1 Track 27

Ex 4.4

Listen to Part 3, Section 3 again and complete the notes in as much detail as you think is necessary.

Section 3

The written agreement between the franchisor and franchisee should specify very clearly what performance and quality standards are expected, and much of the initial training will be ensuring that staff have the skills to achieve these standards. However, regular visits to franchise units are essential in ensuring that the standards are being applied consistently and uniformly, and ongoing training may be necessary to deal with issues that are uncovered in these visits. Protecting the brand is ultimately in the interests of both the franchisor and the franchisee because, for the franchisee, one of the main advantages in running a franchise is that they are buying into and helping to consolidate an established brand.

CD1 Track 28

Ex 5.3

Listen to the sentences and write in the missing prefix to each word.

1. All trade unions were declared illegal by the government.
2. This is one example of a mismatch between the individual's goals and those of the organization.
3. They found no significant correlation between class size and levels of achievement.
4. Real estate transactions rose by 30% last month.
5. Prices are determined through the interaction of supply and demand.
6. These animals exhibited abnormal behaviour compared to the control group.

CD1 Track 29

Ex 5.4

Listen to the sentences and complete them with two to four words in each space.

1. We had to get the photos enlarged because the detail was not very clear on the original ones.
2. Many doctors work long, irregular hours, which puts them under a lot of stress.

3. Crime prevention is an important aspect of the police's work, but it is often difficult to assess its effectiveness.

4. Doctors have noticed an increase in eating disorders, such as bulimia and anorexia, not just among young women but, surprisingly, among young men.

5. These plants should be grown in partial shade, rather than in direct sunlight.

6. Researchers have found that inexperienced drivers are much more likely to be involved in traffic accidents.

CD1 Track 30
Ex 5.5

Listen to the groups of sentences. Complete the sentences with two to four words in each space.

1. a. Children need a secure environment in which to grow up.
   b. Many immigrants are only able to find low-paid, insecure jobs.
   c. The money was invested in securities and property.

2. a. Achievement levels vary considerably from school to school in the city.
   b. Some economists believe that interest rates can be predicted by examining key economic variables.
   c. In the Eden Project they have managed to create a wide variety of habitats.
   d. There is significant variation in access to health care in different parts of the country.

3. a. How are we going to solve this problem?
   b. You need to dissolve the pesticide in water before applying it to the crop.
   c. There appears to be insoluble conflict between the two countries, despite years of peace negotiations.

4. a. A mass spectrometer was used to analyze the gases.
   b. Further analysis of the data is needed to confirm these initial findings.
   c. The course is designed to help students to develop their analytical skills.

5. a. The results indicate that the virus mutates more rapidly than was first believed.
   b. All the main economic indicators suggest that the economy is recovering.
   c. The strike was indicative of the level of the workers' frustration.

6. a. Chomsky was a fierce critic of Bush Senior's foreign policy.
   b. There was some criticism of the way the election had been administered.
   c. The negotiations were critical to the establishment of peace in the area.

Unit 4: Note-taking: Part 1

CD1 Track 31
Ex 2.2

Listen to the recording and read the extract from the transcript at the same time.

Britain's transport problems
Part 1

So Britain's roads, and especially those in the south-east, are overcrowded. There are too many cars on the roads, and at particular times of the day and in particular places, traffic is either very slow or at a standstill. Now, this has a number of effects. Firstly, there is the economic effect, all the time wasted in traffic jams, which means a loss of productivity. Then there's the environmental effect. Cars produce a lot of pollution, which damages the local environment, but it also contributes to global warming. And there's also an effect on people's health. In addition to the poor air quality and the damage this causes people's lungs, the stress of being stuck in traffic each day leads to higher risk of heart disease.

CD1 Track 32
Ex 2.5

Listen to Parts 2–5 of the lecture and make notes on page 34.

Part 2

So, how do we deal with this problem? It is widely accepted among researchers and policy makers that there isn't just one simple solution. For example, it's generally agreed that simply building more roads is not the solution, as research shows that this just leads to an increase in traffic and, in the long term, it worsens the problems I have just described. So, what is needed is a whole range of measures aimed at improving the transport system. The problem is that changes in transport policy take many years to plan and implement. Transport is a politically sensitive issue, so when governments change, then the policy often changes too. This makes it difficult to bring about major changes in policy.

CD1 Track 33
Part 3

Between 1997 and 2010, the Labour government in power at the time adopted an integrated transport policy. What we mean by integrated, is that different aspects of the transport system – so road, rail, air travel – are planned in relation to one another. One of the main issues addressed by that government was how to encourage car drivers to drive less, and to use public transport more. The first point is that just making improvements to the public transport system is not enough to get drivers to use buses or trains. We can provide more buses and trains so that these are less crowded, and we can make them cleaner, safer environments to travel in, and all this will need investment of course, but, even if we do all this, drivers will still prefer to use their cars.

CD1 Track 34
Part 4

So the Labour government tried a number of measures aimed at encouraging drivers to use public transport more. The government tried to encourage car-sharing, so, in some experimental projects on crowded roads, lanes have been designated for use by cars with more than one occupant; CCTV cameras are used to police the trials. The thinking is that if people believe that they can get to work more quickly by driving in this faster lane, then they are more likely to share cars.

In London, congestion charging has had some success; cars are charged to enter a central zone and again, CCTV cameras linked to a computer system are used to ensure compliance. This reduces the number of cars in the centre of London, and the income from congestion charging is then invested in London's public transport system. This is an example of what is meant by an integrated policy.

CD1 Track 35
Part 5

The problem with many of these schemes is that they put pressure on motorists, on drivers. Drivers have already felt under pressure because of the dramatic increases in fuel prices. When the coalition government came to power in 2010, it promised to 'end the war on the motorist'. It was less interested in the schemes to encourage people to drive less, so, for example, the congestion charge zone has been reduced in size. The coalition is more interested in projects to develop the rail network, including a high-speed rail line connecting the north and south of England, and in responding to the growth in air travel either by building a new airport or developing an existing one.

So this shows some of the difficulties involved in encouraging people to drive less and use public transport more, but to sum up the point I made earlier, a whole range of measures attacking the problem from different angles is more likely to be successful than one 'big idea'.

CD1 Track 36
Ex 3.2

In Part 1 of the extract, the lecturer is discussing the reasons for rapid economic growth in East Asia in the 1990s. Listen and continue the following notes.

The East Asian economic miracle
Part 1

And a lot of time was spent in the 1990s trying to interpret the so-called 'East Asian miracle'. There are big disputes about the extent to which the East Asian miracle shows that market liberalism works, particularly when you realize that one of these countries is China, with a highly controlled economy indeed. The Japanese have never run a purely free-market economy. Neither have the Koreans. On the other hand, Singapore, Hong Kong, were swashbuckling free-market capitalism. So there were debates about the extent to which state intervention in the free market pushed forward the East Asian miracle.

CD1 Track 37
Ex 3.3

In Part 2 of the extract, the lecturer goes on to discuss another factor. Listen to Part 2 and continue the notes.

Part 2

But nobody disagreed about one element of the East Asian miracle, and that was investment in people. Country after country in East Asia, it was argued, had undertaken reasonably equitable investments in health care, education and training of people in those countries. And it was argued that this was a major stimulus to industrialization in this area, that you could always hire a lot of people at low labour rates, but who were in reasonably good health, who were literate and who had reasonable skills.

And that was the difference between East Asia and, for example, Africa and Latin America. Or a difference, for that matter, between East Asia and South Asia.

CD1 Track 38
Ex 4.1

Listen to this extract from Track 37. The main stressed words in this sentence are marked in bold.

…, that you could **always** hire a lot of people at **low** labour rates, but who were in reasonably good **health**, who were **literate** and who had reasonable **skills**.

CD1 Track 39
Ex 4.2

Listen to the following sentence from Track 36.

The Japanese have never run a purely free-market economy. Neither have the Koreans.

CD1 Track 40
Ex 4.3

Listen to the extract and complete the sentences with two to seven words in each space.

You need to pre-test the questionnaire. This is really important. Those of you, some of you, will be doing this for, you know, your dissertation. Some of you, I know, are collecting primary data. You need to pre-test the thing, because you're the researcher. You're very close to the subject. You know what you're talking about, but you've got to check that other people do as well. And if you want a statistically valid sample of a hundred or two hundred people, then you've got to make sure that you're collecting the data properly. And it's here that these pre-tests, or pilots, they're going to tell you whether it's going to work or not.

So make sure that you do pilots and, you know, this can be, sort of, half a dozen different people that you question. I mean, you'll soon find out whether you've got any potential … or any doubts about the length of the questionnaire, or the style of particular questions, or whether the sort of questions that you're asking are valid. You'll soon find out from that. So, piloting or pre-testing is really important.

Unit 5: Note-taking: Part 2

CD1 Track 41
Ex 3.1

Listen to a lecturer talking about language learning. Continue the following notes.

Extract 1
Purposes of education

Three very broad perspectives from Littlewood, on the purposes of education. One is a very traditional one: to pass on value, knowledge and culture. So that you see education as passing from the previous generation down to the next generation – the knowledge they will need. Another purpose of education is to prepare learners as members of society. So you have needs which you feel your society must fulfil, and you view education as a vehicle for doing this. And that will influence how language is taught – we'll see how in a moment. And the third view, which is much more humanistic, a humanistic view of education, is where you see learners as individual selves who must be developed. And the process of education as being developing the self – bringing out the individual's best characteristics, allowing them to learn and to fulfil their potential.

CD1 Track 42
Ex 3.2

Listen and continue the following notes.

Extract 2
World economy

What you have to understand is that from the early 1970s onwards there was this primary boom and there were signs of inflation in the world economy. In 1971, America left the gold standard. The value of the dollar had been linked to the value of gold and suddenly the government decided to cut it free. It was effectively devalued. Remember, in 1970, the American economy made up about a third of the total product of the world economy. Today it's about 25% or even less than that, but then the dollar had an even greater influence on the world economy.

So, before the 1970s, we had fixed exchange rates, but from 1971, America devalued the dollar and the exchange rates floated. And from that moment onwards, the major industrial economies, which in the '50s and '60s had had inflation rates of 1%, 2%, 3% per year, suddenly found themselves with inflation rates running at 10%, 15%, 20%. None of you in this room will believe me, probably, when I tell you that, in 1971, Britain's inflation rate was 25%, yes. I can hardly believe that as the words come out of my mouth, and I can remember the year very, very distinctly.

CD1 Track 43
Ex 4.2

Listen to this extract from a lecture entitled *Health in the UK* and make notes.

Health in the UK
OK, so we've looked at some of the problems in the developing world.

What I would like to do now is look at the health situation in the developed world, with particular reference to the United Kingdom. I think the situation can be summarized briefly like this: firstly, life expectancy – how long people are living – is increasing. Secondly, we are taking more and more drugs and as a result of this we are curing, or at least controlling, many illnesses. However, what we are not doing as well as we should is stopping people getting sick in the first place.

Let me just illustrate this point with some statistics.

I've said that life expectancy in the UK is increasing and that's true. For example, let's look at men aged between 35 and 74. The number of men in this age group who died dropped by 42% between 1990 and 2000. Now that's a huge fall. Forty-two per cent fewer deaths in this age group over a ten-year period. Now, it is clear to me that much of this fall has been due to the amount of drugs we take now to cure problems.

If we look at heart disease, for example, and the drugs we take to regulate or 'cure' it, we can see that the number of prescriptions issued by doctors has almost quadrupled – increased by just under 400% – in the last 20 years. This includes drugs to lower blood pressure and to reduce cholesterol. So we really are becoming a nation of pill takers but – and this is the point that I want to emphasize – we are not attacking the underlying causes of heart disease. One major cause of heart disease is physical inactivity. And, in the UK, we are becoming more inactive; we are taking less physical exercise. If you have a look at the statistics on your handout, you will see that these illustrate that since the 1970s the average number of

miles travelled on foot has dropped by around a quarter, just about 23%, and the number of miles travelled by bike has dropped by one-third. In other words, we are walking less, we are cycling less. By contrast, the number of miles people drive has increased by 70% over the same period of time. So, more use of the car and less physical exercise is the overall picture.

Add to this inactivity an unhealthy diet and the results are disastrous. Look at the figures for obesity in the UK. The percentage of obese adults has almost doubled in the last 12 years; a rise of about 92%. So, as a nation, we are becoming more obese as a result of poor diet and a lack of regular physical activity. And what does this mean in terms of life expectancy? Well, over 180,000 people die every year as a result of heart disease. And a third of these deaths – so, more than 60,000 deaths – according to the British Heart Foundation, are premature. In other words, people are dying earlier than they should do.

So, here in the UK we could do more. Other counties are already doing more. For instance, in the last ten years of the 20th century, Norway witnessed a drop of 54% in the number of deaths in men aged between 35 and 74. And, as we saw earlier in that same age group, Britain has a figure of 42%. So, although that seems good, we could and we should be doing more, and we should be looking at how to prevent heart disease rather than concentrating only on how to cure it.

CD1 Track 44
Ex 5.1

Listen and complete the sentences.
1. The government has introduced tax incentives to encourage investment in this region.
2. For tax purposes these organizations are often regarded as charities.
3. A number of reforms to the tax system have been proposed.

CD1 Track 45
Ex 5.2

Read the explanation below and listen to the examples.

add up

What are these?

the main objective

do anything

try out

no idea of it

next day

rapid growth

CD1 Track 46
Ex 5.3

Listen to the phrases. Mark the phrases with the symbols from Ex 5.2.

1. they invested in property
2. a mixture of oil and residues
3. it's an open market
4. it's due on Friday morning
5. free admission on Sundays
6. it shows as a white mark

CD1 Track 47
Ex 5.4

Listen and complete the text with two to five words in each space.

Real options

I'm going to go through the theory of real options, and then I'm going to show you how they can be used to raise some money, particularly on property assets. 'Real options' is a term which was coined ten or 15 years ago, when people began to realize that net present value isn't the only thing you should look at in valuing assets, that a number of assets in companies have a great deal of option value. And so the option theory you've been looking at can also be applied to real assets instead of just financial assets. And that, in raising money, companies particularly have a lot more to offer from an option pricing perspective than they first thought. The idea of real options is that management is not just a passive participant, but that management can take an active role in making and revising decisions that can lead on from unexpected market developments such as, for example, the price of oil has gone up from about $85 a barrel to in excess of $100 a barrel over the last year. So, if you were an oil producer this time last year, you would be taking a very different view on the market for oil. So the increase in oil prices has uncovered a stream of options which make oil producers a lot more valuable, and now you can bring oilfields back on stream that were not necessarily economic. So this is the kind of idea that when we're looking at a project, we're not just looking at a static cash flow, we're actually looking at a cash flow that can be subject to a lot of optionality.

Unit 6: Introducing new terminology

CD2 Track 1
Ex 2.1

Listen to the extract and make notes.

Embedded words

I've been doing some research on one particular problem that arises out of this, and I'd like to use that as a kind of a peg to hang this issue on, to tell you a little bit about it and where we've been getting with this. It's the problem sometimes called the problem of embedded words. So, when we hear a word of several syllables like *responsibility*, a word like *responsibility* invariably contains several smaller English words. So in the case of *responsibility*, we have – you can see here – *response*, *sponsor*, you have *ability* at the end there, and *bill* in the middle there and there's a few others, if you looked hard enough you'd find some more. But almost any word in the English language that has more than two syllables will invariably contain within it, packaged up inside it, smaller English words. Now, consider what the brain is faced with if somebody produces a sentence containing the word *responsibility*. And if the brain wrongly segments *responsibility* into *response* and *ability*, the decoding of that sentence is going to go catastrophically wrong. You see the point I'm making. So when we hear *responsibility*, it's that word; it's not a combination of *response* and *ability*.

CD2 Track 2
Ex 3.2

Listen to the extract and complete the table.

European Union regulations and directives

OK, so the two types of law I want to talk to you about today are directives and regulations, and these are very different, both in the way they are introduced and also in their scope, in the sense that one of them is more concerned with more serious matters while the other is more concerned with minor technical matters. Anyway, I'll return to this in a moment and give you more details and more examples, but before I do that, I want to remind you of some of the key players in the EU as far as law-making is concerned. You might remember – I hope you remember – that there is the European Commission, and the Council of

Ministers and the European Parliament, and all these have a role in law-making. The European Commission is a non-elected organization, which is responsible for the day-to-day running of the EU. You can think of it as a civil service, or the administrators if you like, also called the 'bureaucrats of Brussels', which is where the Commission is based. Then you have the Council of Ministers, which consists of one minister from each of the member states, so these are ministers who are part of the government in their own countries. Do you remember this? Yes? No? But that's clear, yeah, it is? Good. And finally we have the European Parliament, which consists of members who are elected in their own countries to work as full-time MEPs, that is Members of the European Parliament.

So, what roles do these organizations play in law-making and what is the difference between regulations and directives?

Well, first, regulations. So, regulations come either directly from the Commission or from the Council of Ministers and they tend to be concerned with pretty minor technical matters, for example, how much beef there needs to be in a beef sausage, for example or, how much real cream there has to be in ice cream. But they are not all trivial and unimportant things. There are regulations about standards of security in EU passports, for example.

And these regulations come into force as soon as they are published in what is called the *Official Journal*. So in other words, on the same day that these regulations are published, people in all the member states have to observe them, unless, and this is very important, unless individual member states have opted out of that particular area covered by the regulation. Yeah? Let me give you an example of what I mean by opting out. Both the UK and Ireland decided that they wanted to keep control of the whole area of visas and political asylum so they opted out. They said we will not be covered by EU regulation about those issues, yeah so that's fine. So that's regulations. Now what about directives? Well, there are two main differences. The first is that directives have to be accepted first by the Council of Ministers. The Commission cannot do this on its own and the European Parliament cannot do this on its own. Directives can only come from the Council of Ministers. And even then the directive does not become legally binding in any member state until the parliament of that state introduces domestic laws to give the directive effect. So, for

example, the directive comes from the Council of Europe, but it does not automatically become law in Britain, for example. It is only legally binding, it only has legal effect, when the British parliament passes a British law. So it is not the case that we are governed by European laws – many people believe that to be the case, but it is simply not true. There have to be British laws. Is that clear? I know it's a bit complex.

CD2 Track 3
Ex 4.3

Listen to the extract and make notes on the lecturer's definitions of both terms.

Market dominance and monopoly

What do I mean by making the distinction between market dominance and monopoly? We all know what a monopoly is, don't we? It's a single-firm case where the firm is in sole control of a market, and it's protected by such high entry barriers that its position is not vulnerable to competition. It's very rare in the real world for such firms to be in that happy position of being a complete monopoly. In the real world, however, you very often find that you have an approximation to dominance. Now, I've got an example … just looking for a single piece of paper. Oh, here we are. I undertook a study in the mid-'80s and it was quite easy for me to find 22 markets. The period covered, by the way, was mid-'70s to mid-'80s. It was quite easy to find a number of markets where the first firm had a share of 50% or above. In some cases much higher; closer to sort of 80 or 90% even. And the second-largest firm, or firms, were only half or less of the size, in terms of market share, of the dominant firm. So, although in many cases in the real world, you don't have monopoly – you only find that usually in the case of natural monopoly – the notion of dominance, as I want to use it, is quite frequent. You do frequently find one firm with a very sizeable market share – as a rule of thumb, if you like, upwards of 50%, sometimes even as high as 80 or 90%. And the second-largest firm, or firms, has a share perhaps under 10%, or a number of smaller firms all of whom have quite small market shares. Now, I therefore mean by dominance that sort of market structure. The size distribution of firms is highly skewed. You've got one firm in pretty much command of the market but a number of other firms operating in the market in competition.

CD2 Track 4
Ex 5.1

Listen to the following pairs of sentences. What is the difference in the pronunciation of the bold words in each pair?

1. a. What time **does** the train leave?
   b. I'm not sure why he's late. He **does** know about the meeting.
2. a. **Some** researchers have taken a different approach.
   b. We've just got time for **some** questions.
3. a. It was heated to 150°C **for** ten minutes.
   b. There are arguments **for** and against GM crop trials.
4. a. I'm not sure what you're getting **at**.
   b. There were **at** least five errors in the programme.
5. a. Increasingly, small memory devices **can** store large amounts of data.
   b. Well, I **can** do it, but I don't want to.
6. a. Oh, are they going to interview **us** as well as the students?
   b. Can you tell **us** what you've found?

CD2 Track 5
Ex 5.3

Listen and complete the extract with three to five words in each space. In each case, at least one of the missing words is a function word.

Multiple-choice questions – dead easy. They reduce interviewer bias; very easy for people to … very easy and fast for people to answer; very easy for data processing. But the argument goes that they are rather difficult to design. The thing about multiple-choice questions is that you are forcing people into certain answers. This is a good reason for piloting. If you have a multiple-choice question and you pilot it, you may find that people are not, they don't put the issue that you're asking them into that particular set of categories that you've imposed. So that's where your pilots and qualitative research will help. Let me just show you an example of this.

Unit 7: What lecturers do in lectures

CD2 Track 6
Ex 2.2

The lecturer talks about four methods of market research in this lecture. Listen and complete the list of methods that she mentions.

Doing market research

These are the four sort of most common ways, not necessarily in order, but if you're thinking of how market researchers collect their information, those are the ways they do it. Computers are being used to support market researchers a great deal more and the whole business of both selling things over the telephone and doing market research over the telephone has become a very important issue in market research and you'll see reference to terms like CATI: computer-assisted telephone interviewing. I think it probably goes without saying now that when you're phoned up and somebody wants to conduct a market research interview with you, they're probably sitting in front of a PC and we'll look at some of the implications of that. But one of the main ones, of course, is that the data entry occurs at the same time as the asking of the questions, so there's huge savings in terms of that and indeed some of the analysis can go on more or less as you're speaking; things like, you know, in questionnaires you'll need to skip from one section to another, well the computer does that automatically. Next week you're going to hear about a technique called 'adaptive conjoint analysis' and this is an analysis method that, as it suggests, sort of adapts to the person who's being interviewed and starts to react or ask different questions depending on the person.

Telephone interviewing is increasing in its coverage, its importance, but in some ways it's postal questionnaires that we want to concentrate on today, because it's postal questionnaires that in a sense have to be the most accurate, because postal questionnaires are the ones where the respondent doesn't have any help at all. There may be follow-ups and you may follow up by telephone and so on, but it's postal questionnaires which need to be the most accurate, if you like.

Personal interviewing in some ways is very good; very high levels of response, because – although you might have told somebody on the street who is trying to hassle you to answer a few questions to go away – the response rate for personal interviews is actually far higher than these other methods. People find it a lot more difficult to turn away somebody who's sort of standing there in front of them. The problem with personal interviews, of course, is that the interviewer is there and the interviewer themselves can bias the results, and I think it's a lesson in research in general that interviewer bias, of course, is to be avoided, but if you've got somebody in person and they say 'Well how about …?' or 'Do you mean …?' and this kind of thing and this is where distortions can come in. So, personal interviews are good – high response rates – but there is the problem of bias and of course they're very expensive, you're employing real people to ask these questions.

Telephone interviewing: less expensive, but a less good response rate and again some problems of bias. There's a problem whenever you're a person who's asking another person questions. There's always a problem of bias because you want people to expand on their answers and you want people to sort of chat about what they're interested in and therefore you have to interact with them and that interaction is what can cause the biases. The alternative is to have a very strict interviewing schedule and a very strict questionnaire, and you do get this particularly on the telephone where, you know, you get this sort of automaton who's actually a person but they're … it's a very stilted kind of interview and some would say that the quality of the data that is collected as a result is not that high. So we're concentrating on postal questionnaires but accepting that you need a good data collection device.

CD2 Track 7
Ex 3.2

Listen to Part 1 of the extract describing how experiments were carried out. Complete the notes.

Social learning
Part 1

So it seems very plausible that monkeys in the wild learn to fear snakes from other monkeys who've already acquired the fear. And Mineka set up an experimental situation where observer monkeys could watch – who were, of course, naïve and didn't fear snakes initially, as you'll see – could watch a demonstrator who previously had learnt fear of snakes, for example, a

wild-caught monkey. And the question is: what would the observers learn from the demonstrator? To explain the procedure before I show you the data, the observers were tested three times. First of all a pre-test when they were still naïve and they'd never seen a demonstrator acting afraid of snakes; a post-test immediately after they'd seen a demonstrator acting afraid of snakes; and then a follow-up three months later, with no intervening training, to see whether whatever they'd learnt was persistent. And the way the observers were tested was in a 'choice circus', which was just a round arena with four objects at the four corners, one of which was a model snake, and the other three were neutral objects, and they simply measured how much time the observer monkey would spend near the snake. If they were not frightened of snakes they'd spend about quarter of the time near the snake and a quarter of the time near the other objects. If they were afraid of the snake, they'd spend very little time near the snake and much, much more time near the other objects. So, how much time they spend near the snake is one measure of fear. The other measure of fear is that they used something called a 'Wisconsin test apparatus', which is an apparatus simply where monkeys have to reach over a gap to get food, and if you put a frightening stimulus in a glass box in the gap, the monkeys will be reluctant to reach over it to get to the food. So in this test they put either a real snake or a toy snake in a glass box and looked to see how slow the observers were to reach over the snake to get a tempting bit of food. And the slower they were and the more disturbed their behaviour, the more frightened they were concluded to be of snakes. So the question is: how did the observers' behaviour change as a function of watching the demonstrators?

CD2 Track 8
Ex 3.4

Listen to Part 2 of the extract. Make notes on the results and the conclusion the speaker draws from the results.

Part 2

What do the observers do? OK, here they are on the pre-test when they're not afraid of snakes at all, and as you can see they divide their time equally between the four stimuli. They show no avoidance of snakes at all at the pre-test. But at the post-test – when they've had an opportunity to watch an observer who is in the presence of a snake and acting frightened – now they behave not as frightened as the demonstrator monkey, but very much more like the demonstrator. They spend a lot of time near the neutral stimulus and very little time near the snakes. So they have acquired a fear of snakes just by watching another monkey. And this fear is just as strong at the three-month follow-up as it was immediately after. So this is evidence that naïve rhesus monkeys who are not afraid of snakes to start off can learn that snakes are dangerous just by watching another monkey. They don't have to be bitten by a snake or attacked by a snake or anything, they can just learn by watching another monkey.

CD2 Track 9
Ex 4.2

Listen to the extract and complete the notes.

Contestable markets
Essentially, what the theory predicts is that if an incumbent firm in such a market tries to raise its price above the marginal cost, an entrant can immediately appear, undercut that price so long as it's in excess of the marginal cost, and still make a profit. So, if the incumbent firm responds and drops its own price to marginal cost, then the new firm, having made a profit previously, can then leave costlessly. The knowledge on the part of the incumbent firm that that is the case – that if it tries to raise its price, or if there are two or three incumbent firms if they try to raise their price, it would immediately provoke entry and the price will then sink to marginal cost – will mean that the incumbent firms will be unable to raise their price above marginal cost. The significance therefore of the notion of perfectly free entry and exit, you can see – well, I hope – it's significant that here was a theory which was saying even if you've got very highly concentrated oligopolies, if these conditions hold, then you needn't worry; there are very, very few policies you need to adopt towards such industries because they will produce a performance which is in line with that of a perfectly competitive market.

My critique, or the critique of others as well, about the theory of perfect contestability is that if you change the assumptions slightly, the predictions change dramatically. It's very unstable. Let me give you an example of how … of what I mean by that. If in a particular market, for example, which a number of people

have said is contestable, if there are inevitable delays between a firm announcing it's coming into the market and actually managing to produce – and if in coming into the market the entrant has to incur some sunk costs – they can only be slight sunk costs. So if there's a delay, a slight delay, between the firm saying 'I will come into the market', the firm has to build up capacity, there's a delay between the announcement and the actual production, and also if there are some slight exit costs – sunk costs – that the firm has to incur to come into the market, then the predictions of the model are dramatically different. An incumbent firm in such a market can charge the monopoly price, or if it's two or three firms they can charge near the monopoly price. They can charge near the monopoly price until the entrant appears. They can then immediately drop their price to the marginal cost. The entrant, having finally come into production, would then make no money, in fact it would make a loss, it would make a loss equal to its sunk costs. If the entrant is aware of that, it would not come into the market. So the sequence is this, that, with slight alterations, if the notion of a perfectly contestable market is not met, if you make slight changes to the assumptions, even though the market may be approximately contestable, it may make a dramatic difference in the prediction because it means that the incumbent firms will continually be able to charge something approaching a monopoly price. Entry will not occur because the entrants will say, 'I have to incur some slight sunk costs to get into this market, and I won't be able to recover them, and I won't make any money because as soon as I appear and produce, the price will collapse to the marginal cost.'

CD2 Track 10
Ex 5.2

Listen to the following short lecture extracts.

1. Earthquakes are a relatively rare occurrence in the United Kingdom, and when they do occur, they are generally of such low magnitude that they are frequently not recognized as such.
2. Although hospital workers may be exposed to fairly low levels of radiation, measures need to be taken to keep exposure to a minimum.
3. Japan emerged from the postwar period with a developed electronics industry, and its emergence on the global consumer

goods market gave European manufacturers strong competition.

4. It is widely assumed that poverty exists only in developing countries, but this assumption has meant the needs of the urban poor in developed countries are often neglected.

5. The particles collide at something near the speed of light and this collision releases massive amounts of energy.

6. A lot of time was spent trying to involve parents in the road safety scheme, because previous experience has shown that the involvement of the local community in such projects is essential to their success.

7. Research has shown that male lions in different parts of Africa behave in different ways when faced with danger. Do environmental factors account for these differences in behaviour?

8. We studied the performance of these financial products over a period of three years, and we found that some perform significantly better than others.

CD2 Track 11
Ex 5.3

Listen to the following short texts and complete them with words or phrases that are synonyms.

1. Many people are worried that young people lack strong role models, and this concern has prompted the police to question the conduct of professional footballers, whose actions may have a significant influence on young men.

2. The USA decided to stay away from the Moscow Olympics in 1980, in protest at the Soviet Union's invasion of Afghanistan. Four years later, the Soviet Union retaliated with its own boycott of the Los Angeles Olympics.

3. Many multinational companies prefer to team up with local enterprises. Such alliances have a number of advantages.

4. The public's perception of the government's handling of the economy was critical. While the economy had in fact grown by 2%, people viewed the high unemployment rate and the government's inability to control strikes as indicators of poor performance.

Unit 8: Digressions

CD2 Track 12
Ex 2.2

Listen and read the extract. Then answer the questions.

My first set of examples come from a – and I'm going to talk about some fairly classic experiments in this lecture, but I would point out before I go on that there is a really excellent chapter on this subject in Shettleworth's book, which is referred to in the reference list for this lecture. Sara Shettleworth has a superb chapter on social learning. It's called 'Learning from others'. It's very up-to-date, very thoughtful, very comprehensive, and I'm just going to mention just a few of the examples that she mentions. But if you seriously want to think about this area, and it involves many complexities, her chapter is a very good place to go. Anyway, some of the best-known work on social learning, or putative social learning, in rats, in animals, are about food preferences. These are examples of learning the significance of stimuli, learning what foods are good to eat and what foods are bad to eat.

CD2 Track 13
Ex 3.1

Listen to Part 1 and make notes on the main points of the lecture.

Questionnaire design
Part 1

Now, I'm going to show you lots of examples of different types of questions that you can ask, and here are some very general design issues, though. Your questions, they need to be precise, as you'll see in a moment. They need to be well-ordered. Incidentally – sorry, I should have mentioned this earlier – the assessment for this course will, I think, be announced next week, formally, but what it's going to be is a case study. Basically you're going to be asked to evaluate, to comment, appraise. And it'll be a case study describing a, sort of, typical market research process, but it will also include data. There will be data that you can analyze to support your case, and you will be able to analyze it, basically, in whatever way that you want. That'll be up to you. Somebody was asking earlier about will we have to do a questionnaire, and they've probably been talking to people last year who did it and where everybody – basically every single individual –

ran a questionnaire and it basically just got out of hand. It was extremely difficult to mark because people were producing huge volumes of stuff. But this session now is just basically to introduce you to how this sort of data is collected, but you won't be doing this as part of the assessment. So, your questions, they need to be precise, and I'm going to show you some examples of good and bad questions in a moment. You need to decide very carefully, I think, on the ordering. I think there's really not an excuse for it these days, in a sense, for getting this part of it wrong and certainly presentation is very important so we'll talk a little bit about presentation and how you're able to order your questions to make sure that you get – well, there's different schools of thought, but – to make sure that you get optimum response.

CD2 Track 14
Ex 4.2

Listen to Part 2 and answer the questions. Then compare your answers with your group.

Part 2

So you've got to set very clear objectives as to what your questionnaire is designed to achieve. You need to say something about how you're going to collect the data, the sorts of question that you're going to have, the way that you word them, the flow of the questionnaire and so on. Obtaining approval is very important. In the university we have a body known as the Ethics Committee. Technically speaking, if you go out, well if you go outside the university to research anything, you need to get the approval of the Ethics Committee. And the Ethics Committee is, in many ways, a very good idea. The university, and indeed any market research body, that doesn't want its name pulled down by the market research process, of course, so we have to, if we're going out and indeed if students are doing projects, we have to get the implicit approval of the Ethics Committee. Sometimes that can come from the head of the department.

But two or three years ago, just for your information, this group was actually a group of undergraduate students, they decided to do a market research project which was part of the assessment for the course. And they were given a free choice as to what subject they wanted to ask people about. And the explicit instruction was that the people they researched should only be members of the course. And this group came and said 'we want to do a kind of a sex

survey'. And what this was, it was actually fairly innocent, although I did say, you know, this must be kept strictly within the group, and it, sort of, well, I won't go into the details, but it was asking various pretty personal questions really. And the next thing I heard, the next thing I heard of it, was somebody called up from – I can't remember where – but they'd actually been accosted by one of these students somewhere downtown and been asked these questions. And as you can imagine we got into a little bit of trouble about it, and we hadn't cleared it, I hadn't cleared it basically with the committee, because it wasn't, well, I didn't believe it was going out – I didn't think it was going outside. So, anyway, there are, obviously very potential problems in that, but you do need to obtain approval. There is a Market Research Society code of practice on asking questions, on how to do research.

You need to pre-test the questionnaire. This is really important. Those of you, some of you, will be doing this for, you know, your dissertation. Some of you, I know, are collecting primary data. You need to pre-test the thing, because you're the researcher. You're very close to the subject. You know what you're talking about. But you've got to check that other people do as well. And if you want a statistically valid sample of a hundred or two hundred people, then you've got to make sure that you're collecting the data properly. And it's here that these pre-tests, or pilots, they're going to tell you whether it's going to work or not.

So make sure that you do pilots and, you know, this can be, sort of, half a dozen different people that you question. I mean you'll soon find out whether you've got any potential … or any doubts about the length of the questionnaire or the style of particular questions, or whether the sort of questions that you're asking are valid. You'll soon find out from that. So, piloting or pre-testing is really important.

CD2 Track 15
Ex 5.2

Listen to the extract. Which of the activities in 5.1 did the lecturer mention?

Now here's an idea out of the 70s, IRD – integrated rural development. This was the idea that when you worked in rural areas with the poor, and the smallholder and so on, what you tried to do was deliver a package of assistance across the sectors, on the grounds this would give you synergy.

Now just to give you a fairly exaggerated example, if you're trying to get people to plant new varieties of rice and use fertilizer to increase their yields, which you hope is a scale-neutral technology that can be used by smallholders, then why not at the same time combat malaria, inoculate people against disease, clean up the water supply? Because all of these will give you better health, which is a good thing in itself but, of course, healthier farmers can work harder in the fields and so that complements the agricultural measures. And while we're at it, we're going to build some new access roads, because that will improve price relatives at the farm gate and reduce isolation. And while we're at it, we'll run an adult literacy campaign, because literate farmers can read the labels on fertiliser packs, and so on and so forth.

So there was the idea that you should try and do things in development in an integrated fashion across all sectors, because you get synergy, and you get more than the sum of the parts going on. Now integrated rural development was very, very exciting to work in. You got all kinds of things to have a go at, and you've got quite a lot of resources to play with, but these resources were limited compared with needs. So what happened with integrated rural development was within any country, what you did was you took a country, and a country might look just like that, and it might have its capital there, and you take a country that looks just like that, and you do integrated rural development and you do it there, there, there, there, there, oh and there. And yes, that is to scale yes, that is to scale. In other words, you get these little enclaves of very small areas, where donors are putting in resources and everything is done.

And in the early 1970s, Kenya had six small integrated rural programmes, which were very, very well documented and some contemporary, very influential thinkers about development worked on those projects in the early 1970s. But look how tiny they are. That really is to scale. These things were in very small areas indeed. Why? Because, although you could target resources for a small area, you couldn't have the whole country running the kind of programmes that were run there. So because you did everything in integrated rural development, you could only do it on a small scale, concentrated in particular areas.

Now those six small experiences, I think, were all successes. They were successes, but I think, with the benefit of hindsight, we would have to say that they were unrepeatable and institutionally unsustainable. When the donors got bored, and the funds ran out, and the foreign experts' contracts ended, and the Land Rovers began to rust, these projects essentially stopped. Indeed, I arrived in this part of Kenya in 1979, which had been the administrative headquarters, and there were two or three filing cabinets chock-a with files in my room. And I left them there for a while, and then one day I thought, what on earth? And I went through these filing cabinets, and it was sort of all the stuff on, sort of, four or five years, ten years earlier, of the implementation of this. Minutes, plans, documents, contracts, budgets, semi-annual reports, monthly reports, all this kind of stuff. And I looked at this, and I said, my goodness, this is a vital bit of development history here, but it's clogging up my office. So it all went in the skip. There's never, never enough historians around to document these experiences, and that's the sort of way. And as I threw them into the skip, I thought, well there you go, good idea at the time, good people working on it, quite a success, but not sustainable.

CD2 Track 16
Ex 6.1

Listen and complete the notes.
I think that realism excludes the possibility – and it's a growing one – that states can simply isolate themselves from the outside world. The growth of television, the growth of mass communications, have meant that it's virtually impossible for states to ignore what's going on around them, and public opinion has become more important in some respects within states, forcing states to do things that they might not otherwise do. So the strict application of power in terms of maintaining the hierarchy, of ignoring the interests of others, is simply slowly being withered away.

CD2 Track 17
Ex 6.3

Listen and complete the notes.
Ten years later, therefore, we have the Scandinavian ideas impacting on British office design. Another illustration of that might be, you'll discover in the course of the lecture, that some of the factors which are driving the unusual, sometimes, configuration of

office buildings on the Continent, not always but sometimes, are to do with employment legislation – workers' councils, employers' rights, employees' rights.

CD2 Track 18
Ex 6.5

Listen and complete the notes.
Nineteen eighty-two. None of the commercial banks gave any money to the developing world for the best part of ten years after the '82 debt crisis. They got such a bad fright by the debt crisis they more or less ceased lending to the developing world. So the only people who were lending money to governments in the developing world from 1982 onwards were other governments, other aid agencies and other multilateral agencies like the IMF and the World Bank.